MW01124872

Especially for

....

From

....

Date

....

READ
AND
PRAY

THROUGH THE BIBLE

IN A YEAR
FOR TEEN GUYS

© 2024 by Barbour Publishing, Inc.

Written and compiled by Jean Fischer; editorial assistance by Lee Warren.

ISBN 978-1-63609-731-2

All rights reserved. No part of this publication may be reproduced or transmitted for commercial purposes, except for brief quotations in printed reviews, without written permission of the publisher. Reproduced text may not be used on the World Wide Web.

Churches and other noncommercial interests may reproduce portions of this book without the express written permission of Barbour Publishing, provided that the text does not exceed 500 words and that the text is not material quoted from another publisher. When reproducing text from this book, include the following credit line: "From *Read and Pray through the Bible in a Year for Teen Guys: 3-Minute Devotions and Prayers for Morning and Evening*, published by Barbour Publishing, Inc. Used by permission."

Unless otherwise indicated, all scripture quotations are taken from the New Life Version copyright © 1969 and 2003 by Barbour Publishing, Inc. All rights reserved.

Scripture quotations marked NIV are taken from the HOLY BIBLE, NEW INTERNATIONAL VERSION®. NIV®. Copyright © 1973, 1978, 1984, 2011 by Biblica, Inc.™ Used by permission. All rights reserved worldwide.

Published by Barbour Publishing, 1810 Barbour Drive, Uhrichsville, Ohio 44683, www.barbourbooks.com

Our mission is to inspire the world with the life-changing message of the Bible.

Member of the
Evangelical Christian
Publishers Association

Printed in China.

READ
AND
PRAY
THROUGH THE BIBLE
IN A YEAR
FOR TEEN GUYS

3-MINUTE DEVOTIONS & PRAYERS
FOR MORNING & EVENING

BARBOUR
PUBLISHING

WELCOME TO THE BIBLE— GOD'S WORD!

The Bible is the ultimate guidebook for your life (Matthew 4:4), with words that are always true (Psalm 33:4) and powerful (Hebrews 4:12). The Bible is God's gift to you (2 Timothy 3:16). It will teach you how to live (2 Timothy 3:16–17), lead you in God's way (Psalm 119:105), and help you live a pure life (Psalm 119:9). The Bible is forever (Isaiah 40:8; Matthew 24:35). It can provide you with wisdom (Proverbs 2:6), truth (John 8:32; 17:17), strength (Deuteronomy 8:3), and hope (Psalm 119:114; 130:5). It can even help save your soul (James 1:21) with the promise that you can enjoy eternal life in heaven after you die (John 3:16). God wants you to think about His Word all the time so you can become successful and wise (Joshua 1:8). The more you read the Bible, the more you will grow in knowing God and loving Him. Are you ready to begin a year-long, life-changing adventure? Let's get started!

GOD'S PERFECT CREATION

(Genesis 1)

MORNING PRAYER

Creator God, I see Your power in mountains. I hear Your peace in the sound of waves on the shore. I feel Your love in a hyperactive puppy. As I think about all the amazing things You made, I want to know more about You. I pray for everyone who doesn't know You. Please open their eyes to see You, not only in the beauty of Your creation but everywhere! Amen.

EVENING DEVOTION

God saw all that He had made and it was very good.
GENESIS 1:31

Genesis 1 speaks of the perfect world God created. But the world didn't stay perfect. People did things to displease God. This was called sin. God knew that people on their own could never be perfect, so He sent His Son, Jesus, with a plan to save them from their sin. God loves us all so much that His goal is to make us good and pure. He wants to use us to help make His world a better place.

DAY 2

GENESIS 3–4
MATTHEW 2
PSALM 2

LISTEN UP
(Matthew 2)

MORNING PRAYER

Wonderful Counselor, I have a lot to learn about staying still and emptying my mind of distractions so I can be ready to listen. I thank You that I hear Your voice as I read and think about Your Word. I'm thankful that You know the path my life will take and that You are already preparing me. Please help me to stay focused on You. I want to hear all You have to say. Amen.

EVENING DEVOTION

"But as for Me, I have set My King on Zion, My holy mountain." I will make known the words of the Lord. He said to Me, "You are My Son. Today I have become Your Father. Ask of Me, and I will give the nations for you to own. The ends of the earth will belong to You."

PSALM 2:6–8

God saw the world filling with sin, but He had a plan. He sent Jesus and made Him King and ruler over all the earth. After Jesus was born and the magi came bringing Him gifts, they knew He was the King who would reign over all nations. His birth was just the beginning of God's plan to save us from sin. You'll learn more about God's plan as you read through the Bible this year. It's a powerful and amazing story!

TODAY'S GIFT
(Psalm 3)

MORNING PRAYER

Lord God, You never sleep. Every night You stay with me. Each day is Your gift to me. I will thank You for every minute. I'll give today my best. If obstacles get in my way, I trust You will show me what to do. You will keep me strong and protect me if trouble comes. Because You are always with me, tonight I will lie down and rest, knowing that You will watch over me. Amen.

EVENING DEVOTION

He said, "Be sorry for your sins and turn from them! The holy nation of heaven is near."
MATTHEW 3:2

People turned away from God and lived in ways that displeased Him, so God sent a great flood. He saved only Noah, his family, and pairs of every kind of animal. But people kept sinning. God hates sin; still, He wants us to be saved from His punishment. That's why He sent Jesus to die on the cross and take the punishment we deserve. If you are sorry for your sins and turn to Jesus, you can be sure God will forgive you.

DAY 4

GENESIS 8–10
MATTHEW 4
PSALM 4

PEACEFUL SLEEP
(Genesis 8:21–22)

MORNING PRAYER

Dear God, after the flood, Noah prayed and You provided him with everything he needed. I'm thankful that You understand me and give me what I need. You know my every thought, both good and evil; You know the things that make me afraid. You provide for me even when I am weak and unsure of myself, sometimes even before I ask. How could I not want to follow You, God? Amen.

EVENING DEVOTION

*I will lie down and sleep in peace. O
Lord, You alone keep me safe.*
PSALM 4:8

Nothing on earth can make you truly safe. But when you trust in Jesus, you can rest comfortably, feeling secure because you know that He, the ruler of the universe, cares for and loves you. And someday when you die, you will be safe forever, living with God in heaven. So sleep peacefully, knowing that nothing can touch you outside of God's will. He is faithful and He dearly loves you. You are His son.

GOD LISTENS
(Psalm 5)

MORNING PRAYER

Lord God, I look forward to meeting with You every day. I pray, feeling confident that You will protect me. Teach me to love You first and most, and then to love others as I want to be loved. And when I'm not sure what to do, show me the way. Lead me on the right path. Guide me to follow Your way even when the eyes of my heart can't see it. Amen.

EVENING DEVOTION

In the morning, O Lord, You will hear my voice. In the morning I will lay my prayers before You and will look up.
PSALM 5:3

Pray with confidence that God will hear you, and then listen and watch for His answer. Get in the habit of starting each day in conversation with Him. When you talk with God in the morning, you will be more aware of Him all through your day. Pray for the small things and the big things, knowing not only that God will listen to you but that He will always act to give you exactly what you need.

PRAY AND LOVE

(Matthew 5:44)

MORNING PRAYER

Dear Lord, I confess I don't always feel like loving my enemies. But *pray* and *love* are actions You want me to take no matter what I'm feeling. And You know what happens when I pray for my enemies. My feelings toward them change. So as I pray for them, I ask for eyes to see them as *You* see them. Let me pray in a loving way, trusting You with the outcome. Amen.

EVENING DEVOTION

He took him outside and said, "Now look up into the heavens and add up the stars, if you are able to number them." Then He said to him, "Your children and your children's children will be as many as the stars." Then Abram believed in the Lord, and that made him right with God.

GENESIS 15:5–6

Abraham had no children. His wife was too old to have a baby, and they certainly would have been past the point of hoping for such a miracle. Nothing would have made Abraham think he could have a never-ending line of descendants. But God promised Abraham as many descendants as there are stars. Abraham's faith in God made him set aside what he believed and instead trust in God's promise. Do you have faith as strong as Abraham's?

WHAT IF?
(Genesis 18:22–32)

MORNING PRAYER

Lord, Abraham begged You to spare the sinful city of Sodom if You could find only ten righteous people there. First, he asked for a little. Then he kept asking for more, and You answered yes. You've done the same for me. When I've asked for a little, You were ready to give more. When I pray for others, remind me of that. Prepare me to see even bigger blessings than I expect. Amen.

EVENING DEVOTION

So Sarah laughed to herself, saying, "Will I have this joy after my husband and I have grown old?" Then the Lord said to Abraham, "Why did Sarah laugh and say, 'How can I give birth to a child when I am so old?' Is anything too hard for the Lord? I will return to you at this time next year, and Sarah will have a son."
GENESIS 18:12–14

Do you ever fail to take God's promises seriously? Maybe you feel you're not worthy of them. Maybe deep down you don't think God cares enough to keep His promises to you. Or maybe you think He isn't powerful enough to actually do what He says. Thankfully, a lack of faith does not affect God's faithfulness. He will always keep His promises, whether or not you believe them. He will prove Himself to you just as He did to Sarah.

DAY 8

IMPORTANT TO GOD
(Psalm 8)

MORNING PRAYER

Lord God, if I were standing at the foot of the tallest mountain, at the edge of the ocean, or on the rim of a volcano, I would feel so insignificant. But the truth is, You made me only a little lower than the angels—crowned with glory and honor and given control over Your creation. That truth makes me want to praise You, praying that all the glory will be returned to You. Amen.

EVENING DEVOTION

*When I look up and think about Your heavens, the
work of Your fingers, the moon and the stars, which
You have set in their place, what is man, that You think
of him, the son of man that You care for him?*
PSALM 8:3–4

How would your life change if you truly understood how important you are to God? God perfectly cares for everything He has created, including birds and flowers (Matthew 6:26–30). As His child, you are much more important than those things. He, the Creator of every star in the sky, is mindful of you! You can trust that you have, and always will have, all that you need under His protection.

WHAT'S BEST FOR YOU
(Matthew 7:7-11)

MORNING PRAYER

Heavenly Father, You give good gifts to Your children when we ask. Asking for help from You is like asking my parent here on earth. You may not give me what I ask for, but You will give me what's best. You know better than I do the answer that fits perfectly into Your plan for me. I thank You that You always know exactly what I need. Amen!

EVENING DEVOTION

Abraham said, "God will have for Himself a lamb ready for the burnt gift, my son." So the two of them walked on together.
GENESIS 22:8

Imagine God asking Abraham something so painful as to give up his son. God let Abraham keep Isaac, and He blessed Abraham for having enough faith to trust Him even when He asked Abraham to do something hard. God gave up His own Son, Jesus, in exchange for our sins. We didn't deserve His gift. God loved us so much He gave us Jesus so our sins would be forgiven forever. That's why we have every reason to trust God just as Abraham did.

DAY 10

GENESIS 24
MATTHEW 7:12–29
PSALM 9:9–20

HE'S WITH YOU. . .ALWAYS
(Psalm 9:10)

MORNING PRAYER

Jesus—that's just one of many names we call You. Emmanuel—You are with me always. Prince of Peace—You are my Comforter. Wonderful Counselor—I seek You when I don't know which way to turn. You are King of kings and Lord of lords. I bow before You. You supply my every need. You will never give up on me, and no one is more powerful than You. Jesus, I put my trust in You. Amen.

EVENING DEVOTION

Those who know Your name will put their trust in You. For You, O Lord, have never left alone those who look for You.
PSALM 9:10

Take time to think about the faithfulness of God in your life. Remember those times when even in the middle of your doubt or fear He showed Himself to you in powerful and visible ways. If you truly know the character and person of God, you will, without a doubt, be ready to put your trust in Him because you know He has never, and will never, let you down.

ANSWERED PRAYERS
(Genesis 25:21–23)

MORNING PRAYER

Lord, from the day when the first boy, Cain, was born to Adam and Eve, You have heard parents praying. You heard Isaac ask You to give his wife, Rebekah, a baby. And then when she was pregnant, Rebekah prayed for her twin boys before they were born. You still hear when parents—all parents and *my* parents—pray, and You will answer them just as You answered Adam, Eve, Isaac, and Rebekah. Amen.

EVENING DEVOTION

*A man with a bad skin disease came and got
down before Him and worshiped Him. He said,
"Lord, if You will, You can heal me!"*
MATTHEW 8:2

The man with the skin disease understood that his healing depended completely on the grace of God. Knowing that God *could* heal him, he didn't place demands on God, beg Him, or even argue with God about why he should be healed. Instead, he worshiped Him by humbly acknowledging His power both to heal and to decide whether to heal. We should have the same attitude, relying on the truth that God is powerful enough to give us strength and make us well.

DAY 12

GENESIS 27:1–28:9
MATTHEW 8:18–34
PSALM 10:12–18

SURPRISES
(Matthew 8:23–27)

MORNING PRAYER

God, like those disciples crossing the Sea of Galilee in their boat, I expect clear sailing with You at my side. If trouble comes, I might think You're not paying attention. But that's not true! You want me to have faith that You will protect me. You are with me always, so I never need to be afraid. Even the winds and waves obey You. Sunshine or rain, You will see me through. Amen.

EVENING DEVOTION

*In this way, You will do the right thing for those without
a father and those who suffer, so that man who is
of the earth will no longer make them afraid.*
PSALM 10:18

When the world's troubles seem so great, it's important to remember that the God who calmed the wind and waves is still the ruler of this earth. One day He will get rid of everything that is evil—forever. God will judge the earth so that people will no longer do bad things and turn against Him. He will make all things right. Don't lose hope. God rules the earth.

GOD CARES
(Matthew 9:27–29)

MORNING PRAYER

Lord, like the religious ruler who worried about his daughter, I've prayed to You about those I love. Like the two blind men, I've asked you to take pity on me. I know You care about me no matter how I feel. I'm grateful that You promise to hear my prayers and that You care. Thank You for loving me, God. Amen.

EVENING DEVOTION

The blind men came to Him. Then Jesus said to them, "Do you have faith that I can do this?" They said to Him, "Yes, Sir!" Then Jesus put His hands on their eyes and said, "You will have what you want because you have faith."
MATTHEW 9:28–29

The Bible is filled with stories of God's caring. In today's reading we discover He loves the unloved (Leah), He sees those who feel helpless (the two blind men), He invites the outcasts (sinners and tax collectors), and He heals the sick and needy (the religious ruler's daughter and the woman with the blood disease). You serve a caring and loving God who does not overlook any of His children. He cares deeply for you.

DAY 14

GENESIS 30:1–31:21
MATTHEW 10:1–15
PSALM 12

MORE LIKE JESUS

(Psalm 12:5)

MORNING PRAYER

Lord, I ask that You make me more like You. Help me to see and hear as if through Your eyes and ears. Make me more like You in the ways I care for and show love to the poor and needy. Your words to me are more valuable than silver. Change my priorities from things to people. Teach me through Your Word so I will know better how to pray. Amen.

EVENING DEVOTION

"Because of the suffering of the weak, and because of the cries of the poor, I will now rise up," says the Lord. "I will keep him safe as he has wanted to be."
PSALM 12:5

The Lord sees your troubles, and He hears when you cry out to Him. He hears all your prayers, and He will act in His own perfect timing. God knows when people treat you unfairly. No matter what they say about you or how they try to hurt you, remember that God is the supreme judge who rules over everything. He loves you forever, and that should matter much more than the way people here on earth treat you.

WORDS
(Matthew 10:18–20)

MORNING PRAYER

Jesus, I want to tell others about You, but sometimes I can't find the words. If a friend asks me about my faith, please give me clear words to say. If someone talks badly about me, give me the right words to respond. I know if I read and study the Bible and live by its truth, I will be ready to honor You with all the words I need. Amen.

EVENING DEVOTION

But I have trusted in Your loving-kindness. My heart will be full of joy because You will save me. I will sing to the Lord, because He has been good to me.
PSALM 13:5–6

You can be like Jacob in Genesis 32 and remind God of His promises when you pray. The Bible is filled with God's promises. Look for them as you read. When you're faced with a scary situation, remember the promises God has made to you and pray them back to Him, like Jacob did. Although God certainly doesn't need to be reminded of the promises He has made, you will be blessed when you are reminded of them.

GENESIS 32:22–34:31
MATTHEW 10:37–11:6
PSALM 14

WRESTLING
(Genesis 32:22–30)

MORNING PRAYER

Lord, sometimes I wrestle with my problems. When I pray, I feel like I'm wrestling with You too! I know You are trying to help me, just like You did Jacob in Genesis 32. When I pray long and hard about something, I need to remember that You don't always lead me in the easiest way, but You change me and strengthen me for what's ahead. I need You, God. Please bless me. Amen.

EVENING DEVOTION

So Jacob gave the place the name of Peniel. For he said, "I have seen God face to face, and yet I am still alive."
GENESIS 32:30

Think about the times when God has shown Himself to you in special or important ways. Unlike Jacob, you probably don't have a permanent limp to always remind you of your meeting with God. But it is still important to remember and celebrate God's faithfulness so that in times of trouble, when you might be tempted to doubt God, you have something solid to look back on to remind you of how He always cares for you.

GOD, YOUR ROCK
(Psalm 15)

MORNING PRAYER

Dear God, I want to be worthy of living with You in Your kingdom, but the requirements are beyond me. How grateful I am that I don't have to be perfect. You sent Jesus to make a way for me to be blameless in Your sight. Through Him, I am a work in progress. I promise to do my best to honor You by doing what is right and good. Amen.

EVENING DEVOTION

O Lord, who may live in Your tent? Who may live on Your holy hill? . . . He who does these things will never be shaken.
PSALM 15:1, 5

Psalm 15 describes the qualities a person would need to be worthy to live with God. It ends by saying a person who has these attributes will always stand strong. When you welcome God into your heart, He lives within you, and you live with Him! He becomes more important to you than any trouble you face. You live your life like you are anchored safe and sound to an immovable Rock.

DON'T WORRY

(Psalm 16)

MORNING PRAYER

Dear Lord, if I can't sleep at night, I turn to You and pray. Talking with You helps me to lock up the thoughts swirling around in my head. You are my Rock, solid and unmoving. You make me feel secure. You provide for all my needs. You give me joy. I have no reason to lie awake worrying. I will rest in You, knowing that whatever happens, You are with me forever. Amen.

EVENING DEVOTION

You will show me the way of life. Being with You is to be full of joy. In Your right hand there is happiness forever.
PSALM 16:11

Throughout your life, God will show you the path to follow. Trust Him to help you with every decision. If a choice seems too difficult, ask God to reveal the next right step. Do your best to serve Him, and you will find that He will guide you, protect you, and make you strong. The more closely you follow Him, the more clearly you will experience His presence. God wants you to have good things in life. He wants you to experience His goodness forever.

ANSWERS FROM GOD

(Genesis 40:8)

MORNING PRAYER

Dear God, I looked forward to reading about Joseph so I could learn from this man who trusted You despite all the troubles he faced. I want to call on You like Joseph did. I want prayer to be such a basic part of my everyday life that I become a reflection of You in everything I say and do. Amen.

EVENING DEVOTION

*Keep me safe as You would Your own eye.
Hide me in the shadow of Your wings.*
Psalm 17:8

You instinctively protect your eyes from harm. When startled, you blink. If something suddenly comes flying in your direction, you immediately shield yourself. Your eyes are valuable, so you take care to protect them. You are precious in God's sight—you are His son and of great value. He will never fail to protect you. God is like a mother bird with her strong wings outstretched to shelter her little ones. Just like that, you can rest safe and sound in the shadow of His wings.

PRAISE GOD

(Matthew 12:34)

MORNING PRAYER

Father God, I'm ashamed by some of the words that come from my mouth. Too often I speak defensively and with anger. I just keep doing it, and I know it's not pleasing to You. I need a heart change! Please fill up my heart with so much of You that whatever comes from my mouth will be as if You are speaking through me with grace, love, and joy. Amen.

EVENING DEVOTION

*Joseph answered Pharaoh, "Not by myself.
God will give Pharaoh a good answer."*
GENESIS 41:16

If you are honored for something you have done, remember to give the praise to God. Everything you accomplish should be an opportunity for you to give Him the credit. God honors humility. True humility is recognizing that your achievements are owed to Him and also to what others have done to get you where you are. So direct the praise to God and to others—that's where it belongs.

YOUR NEXT STEP
(Psalm 18:25–26)

MORNING PRAYER

Lord, when I read the Bible, I see the real me. You come to me where I am and frame your message to fit me. Your pure and perfect Word helps me to understand as You open my eyes to new meanings. Your Word is like a lesson plan written just for me. It helps me with my weaknesses and makes me strong. Lead me to use what I learn to honor You. Amen.

EVENING DEVOTION

*You make my lamp bright. The Lord
my God lights my darkness.*
PSALM 18:28

God knows your future. He planned it out before you were even born. He already knows your path, so ask Him to be like a lamp and light your way. When trouble comes and the way out seems dark, trust God to guide you and help you to see the next step you should take.

GOD'S STRENGTH
(Psalm 18:30–50)

MORNING PRAYER

Dear God, sometimes when things get hard I want You to make them better while I sit on the sidelines doing nothing. But You want me to work *with* You—to act! You give me strength to tackle my problems and overcome them, and when I grow tired, You are my place of rest. I'm ready to do this. Let's work together! When I win over my troubles, I'll give all the credit to You. Amen.

EVENING DEVOTION

"So let your servant stay and work for my lord, instead of the boy. Let the boy go home with his brothers."
GENESIS 44:33

Never assume that someone can't be changed by God's grace. Based on the cruel way Joseph's brothers treated him, it would be easy to think that his brothers were past saving. But Joseph's brother Judah was willing to sacrifice his own life for the sake of his younger brother. That is the sort of amazing sacrifice Jesus made for us—He was willing to give His own life so ours would be saved. God can work in any life. No one is beyond saving.

GOD'S WORD
(Psalm 19)

MORNING PRAYER

Dear God, the Bible is powerful, beautiful, and worth studying. But its words mean nothing if I don't do what it says. Help me to meditate on Your Word and align my behavior with what it teaches. When I'm tired, help me to find rest within its pages. And when I need wisdom, lead me into Your Word to find it. I trust the Bible to contain all the tools I will ever need. Amen.

EVENING DEVOTION

The Word of the Lord is worth more than gold, even more than much fine gold. They are sweeter than honey, even honey straight from the comb. And by them Your servant is told to be careful. In obeying them there is great reward.
PSALM 19:10–11

The Bible is perfect, pure, true, and always right. It opens our eyes to new ideas and draws us closer to God. It brings joy because it is always trustworthy, and its words are forever. It overflows with nuggets of wisdom to discover. God's Word is far more valuable than gold, and we are rewarded when we follow its commands. With such a treasure in your possession, you should make time to read the Bible every day.

GOD'S POWER AT WORK

(Genesis 48)

MORNING PRAYER

Father God, I can only imagine how excited Jacob was to have grandchildren. Grandparents, like Jacob, are wise. They know how to pray for their grandchildren and lead them to You. I thank You for the gift of grandparents and for everyone who prays for me. I hope when I have children and grandchildren of my own, I will know how to pray for them too. I want them to know You! Amen.

EVENING DEVOTION

Now I know that the Lord saves His chosen one. He will answer him from His holy heaven, with the saving power of His right hand.

PSALM 20:6

Psalm 20 is a powerful psalm written by King David. He knew what it was like to be in trouble and have God come to his rescue. Did you know you share that experience with David? Jesus has rescued you from sin. He saved you and He will keep on saving you whenever you face trouble. You know He can be trusted, so don't keep Jesus a secret. Tell the world you belong to Him, and let everyone see His power at work within you.

STRONGER
(Matthew 14)

MORNING PRAYER

Lord Jesus, I want to be like Peter, walking boldly toward You across the waves. But when You call to me, sometimes I hesitate, afraid I can't do what You ask of me. How thankful I am that You understand my weakness. You reach out Your hand and lift me up, safe, secure, and walking again on the pathway toward You. Lord, help me not to be afraid to take that first step. Amen.

EVENING DEVOTION

But the more the Egyptians made them suffer, the more they became until they spread throughout the land.
EXODUS 1:12

The Hebrews' suffering in Egypt did just the opposite of what you might expect—it made them stronger. God is powerful and good. He can take even the worst trouble and use it to build your strength. Maybe you are facing something today that you feel is more than you can handle. Whatever it is, trust God. He is bigger than any problem you face. Ask him for all the strength you need for whatever comes your way.

NOTHING IS TOO DIFFICULT FOR GOD

(Exodus 3)

MORNING PRAYER

God, You told Moses, "I AM WHO I AM" (Exodus 3:14). You are everything! Without You, the world would fall apart. Fill me up with a sense of awe and wonder at who You are. Help me understand Your greatness. I want to follow You for the rest of my life, no matter what happens. I'm grateful that You, the great I Am, will always be with me. Amen.

EVENING DEVOTION

And God said to Moses, "I AM WHO I AM." And He said, "Say to the Israelites, 'I AM has sent me to you.'"

EXODUS 3:14

The beautiful truth of God's power and goodness is woven all throughout history. Don't think that any sin, weakness, or challenging circumstance is too difficult for Him to use for His glory. As an example, in today's Bible reading, God used an evil pharaoh, a "chance" encounter with an Egyptian princess, and a murderer and coward named Moses to accomplish His purposes.

GOD IS SO GOOD
(Matthew 15:32–38)

MORNING PRAYER

Lord Jesus, You know me. Sometimes I'm slow to offer my help to those who need it. But I want to get better at stepping up to help others. Point to a specific person at a specific time with a specific need. Then teach me to act immediately without hesitating. Jesus, make me more like You, ready to act with compassion and love. Amen.

EVENING DEVOTION

"Do you not yet understand or remember the five loaves of bread that fed five thousand men? And how many baskets full were gathered up? Or do you not even remember the seven loaves of bread that fed the four thousand men? And how many baskets full were gathered up?"
MATTHEW 16:9–10

How easy it is to forget God's power and goodness. Moses, afraid of speaking to the people, forgot that God was the one who had created him and who could easily help him speak. Amid the pressure of feeding a crowd, the disciples quickly forgot the miracle that Jesus had already performed to feed thousands. What have you forgotten about God? What do you worry about because you haven't remembered that God is powerful, that He loves you, and that He has a good plan for your life?

EXODUS 5:22–7:24
MATTHEW 16:13–28
PSALM 23

TRUTH
(Exodus 6:28–7:6)

MORNING PRAYER

Father, I'm grateful the Bible provides examples of people of faith with all their faults. As You did for them, you will prepare me for the plans You have for me. If I need help, You will guide me and send others to my aid. Please prepare me for the work You want me to do. With Your guidance, the helpers You will give me, and the Holy Spirit, I will complete the task. Amen.

EVENING DEVOTION

"And I tell you that you are Peter. On this rock I will build My church. The powers of hell will not be able to have power over My church."
MATTHEW 16:18

When you read Psalm 23, read it first for the beauty of its words. Then read it again, noticing that it is packed with many comforting and empowering truths. When you read Matthew 16, notice Jesus' promise: "I will build My church." It speaks of God's power over everything. Nothing can get in the way of His plan. Believing that truth will help you to find courage in all you do and give you a sense of peace.

GOD'S COMFORTING POWER
(Psalm 24)

MORNING PRAYER

Lord, everything in me and everything in the earth and sky belongs to You because You are our Creator. I'm amazed at the miracle of creation, from my DNA to all the laws of nature You put into place. You make everything work in an orderly fashion. You could crush all creation with the wave of a single finger, but instead You love us with unending mercy and grace. Thank You, Lord. Amen.

EVENING DEVOTION

*The earth is the Lord's, and all that is in it,
the world, and all who live in it.*
PSALM 24:1

God made the world and everything in it. He still rules over the earth and all its people. The same powerful God you read about in the Bible still reigns today. His amazing power causes fear in some people. But as one of His children, you can find comfort and courage in His power because it means there is nothing in your life He doesn't have control over. He wants everything for you and about you to be good.

DAY 30

EXODUS 10–11
MATTHEW 17:10–27
PSALM 25

HOPE
(Psalm 25)

MORNING PRAYER

You are the God of hope. You are *my* hope. You are my personal Lord and Savior. You saved me from sin so I can live with You forever. I depend on You twenty-four hours a day. I pray You will help me accept all You want to teach me. My trust in You will never fail because *You* never fail. You will never let me down. Amen.

EVENING DEVOTION

*Then the Lord said to Moses, "Go to Pharaoh. For I
have made his heart and the heart of his servants hard,
so that I may do My powerful works among them. You
may tell your son and your grandson how I made it very
hard for the Egyptians and how I did My powerful works
among them. So you may know that I am the Lord."*

Exodus 10:1–2

God continued to harden Pharaoh's heart—to allow evil inside, which caused trouble for the Israelites. Why did God put His people through this hardship? We can look back on it now and see that God's purposes were to free His people, to show His power to an evil nation, and to start the Israelites on a journey to a beautiful land of their own. You can always rely on God to work out your troubles in ways that honor Him and bring about good.

TRUSTING GOD

(Exodus 12)

MORNING PRAYER

Jesus, Your purpose was to take away the sins of the world. I feel overwhelmed when I think about how You suffered, dying on the cross. You died for me so I can have a place in heaven someday. I can rest now, knowing You took the punishment I deserved. No matter how many times or how many ways I say it, I am so grateful for Your sacrifice. Amen.

EVENING DEVOTION

O Lord, stand by me for I have lived my life without blame. I have trusted in the Lord without changing.
PSALM 26:1

Are you as confident as David was about being found innocent of his sins? Could you ask God to judge you with a clear conscience? David's kind of certainty over when he entered heaven and stood before God that he would be judged blameless of his sins, may seem impossible—and on his own, it was. God's righteousness and forgiveness assured David that God would find him innocent of sin. Thanks to Jesus, you have that confidence too.

DAY 32

EXODUS 13–14
MATTHEW 18:21–35
PSALM 27

STRONG FAITH

(Psalm 27)

MORNING PRAYER

Dear Lord, I thank You for the confidence of knowing that when I reach heaven, I will see how You made my path on earth straight from beginning to end. I look forward to sitting with You and watching in awe as You conduct kingdom business. But for now, I am content seeing Your goodness here on earth. Whatever happens here, I am happy knowing You are with me forever. Amen.

EVENING DEVOTION

But Moses said to the people, "Do not be afraid! Be strong, and see how the Lord will save you today. For the Egyptians you have seen today, you will never see again."
EXODUS 14:13

Moses' trust in God's promise to deliver His people from Egypt was so secure that not even six hundred chariots filled with Egyptian soldiers could shake his confidence. And God did not let Moses down. You serve the same promise-keeping, all-powerful God today. Ask Him to build your faith as strong as that of Moses. Then you too can stand firm, confident God will save you even in the face of overwhelming odds.

GOD'S HELP
(Exodus 15:11)

MORNING PRAYER

Heavenly Father, there is no God like You. In a world that depends on science more than on You, I can see Your greatness all around me as I explore Your creation. Thank You for revealing Yourself, for giving me eyes to see. Continue to improve my spiritual vision, that I might see You more clearly. Whatever You teach me, help me to pass it on to others faithfully. Amen.

EVENING DEVOTION

The Lord is my strength and my safe cover. My heart trusts in Him, and I am helped. So my heart is full of joy. I will thank Him with my song.
PSALM 28:7

Trust in God and you will be helped. Sometimes the way we want God to help is different from the kind of help He provides. But even though it may not feel like it at the moment, the way God decides to help you is infinitely better than anything you could imagine. Can you think of examples in your own life when God helped you in an unexpected way? Praise Him for His faithfulness, goodness, and grace.

DAY 34

EXODUS 17–19
MATTHEW 19:16–30
PSALM 29

TREASURE IN HEAVEN

(Matthew 19:16–30)

MORNING PRAYER

Lord, I praise You for all the blessings I couldn't have predicted or planned for. You know my heart. I say I want to follow You no matter what, but sometimes I fail. Forgive me when I back down. Thank You for giving me strength for today's problems. Help me to face those difficult times when "no matter what," You ask me to follow You. Amen.

EVENING DEVOTION

Jesus said to him, "If you want to be perfect, go and sell everything you have and give the money to poor people. Then you will have riches in heaven. Come and follow Me."
MATTHEW 19:21

Is there anything in your life that you would refuse to give up for the sake of Jesus and His kingdom? In Matthew 19:21, Jesus asked a man to be willing to give up earthly comforts because what Jesus can give is far better than anything this world can offer. It's only in letting go of earthly treasures that you can fully know the wonderful riches He offers to those who choose to follow Him.

JOY
(Psalm 30)

MORNING PRAYER

I praise You, Lord, because when I feel down, You lift me up. You are always ready to save me. In sad times, I look forward to Your promise of better days. I wish every day was marked by blue skies and sunshine. But some days are rainy, dark, and gloomy. Still, they bring growth. Those rainy days make me strong. In fair or foul weather, my joy is found in You. Amen.

EVENING DEVOTION

"Do I not have the right to do what I want to do with my own money? Does your eye make you want more because I am good?"
MATTHEW 20:15

Do you ever question whether God's plan for you is really the best? Do you compare your life to someone else's? Remember, God has the right to do with you as He pleases. He knows better than anyone what is best for you. It is important to believe with all your heart in His goodness. Refuse to compare your blessings to those of others. You will find a true sense of freedom when you accept that God's plan for you is perfect.

DAY 36

EXODUS 22–23
MATTHEW 20:20–34
PSALM 31:1–8

CARE FOR OTHERS
(Matthew 20:26–28)

MORNING PRAYER

Lord Jesus, sometimes I wonder at Your patience with me.
You are God, the one who gave up everything for me—me,
who's no taller than Your fingernail! And yet You welcome
me as a son into Your family, a receiver of all Your heavenly
blessings. Help me to become more like You. Use me as Your
hands, feet, and heart so that when others are with me, they
will see You. Amen.

EVENING DEVOTION

*"Do not bring trouble to any woman whose husband
has died or any child whose parents have died. If you
bring them trouble, and they cry out to Me, for sure
I will hear their cry. My anger will burn and I will kill
you with the sword. Then your wives will lose their
husbands. And your children will lose their fathers."*
EXODUS 22:22–24

The laws in the book of Exodus can sometimes seem tedious
and harsh, but we learn about God's character through His
instructions for the way His people ought to live. His love
and defense of the needy are seen in His warning to anyone who dares harm a widow or orphan. To take advantage
of the weak and vulnerable is no small offense in God's eyes.
God does not overlook those who are so often overlooked
in our world—and neither should we.

NO FEAR
(Matthew 21:21–22)

MORNING PRAYER

Jesus, You say You'll move mountains if I ask in prayer, believing. What are the mountains in my life? If I don't get what I ask for, is my faith at fault? Am I asking for the wrong thing? Am I blind to Your answers? It's not about me. You, God of the impossible, can lift a mountain with a word. Nothing I ask or imagine is too great for You. Help me to believe. Amen.

EVENING DEVOTION

My times are in Your hands. Free me from the hands of those who hate me, and from those who try to hurt me.
PSALM 31:15

How would your life change if you, like David, could truly grasp that your life is in God's hands? Wouldn't that belief give you an unshakable peace and remove any fear? You would know that God allows you to go through trials and will carefully work them out for your good. Remember this when you face any trouble—God's got this! He's got your life in His hands, and He's got the situation under His control.

DAY 38

EXODUS 26–27
MATTHEW 21:28–46
PSALM 31:19–24

WHAT DO YOU BELIEVE?

(Exodus 27:20–21)

MORNING PRAYER

Lord, I feel like my spirit is an oil lamp I need to keep burning, but sometimes I let the supply of oil run out. My light goes dark, forgive me. Your love burns like a light inside me. I thank You that Your supply of oil is endless. Fill me, light my spirit, use me to shine Your light on others. Let my light shine pure and bright again. Amen.

EVENING DEVOTION

Jesus said to them, "For sure, I tell you this: Tax-gatherers and women who sell the use of their bodies will get into the holy nation of heaven before you."
MATTHEW 21:31

Whether or not you are popular here on earth, whether or not you have nice things, whether or not you excel in sports or academics—none of it compares to your status in the kingdom of God. All that matters is your belief in Jesus. You can be encouraged that no matter what you do in your life, you are never beyond saving. And remember that no amount of good you do in life will get you into heaven if you don't believe that Jesus died on the cross for your sins.

WHEN LIFE IS HARD
(Matthew 22:8–10)

MORNING PRAYER

Dear God, who am I that You invited me to live with You forever in heaven? When He died for me, Jesus saved my soul. All You ask is that I accept Him so that when I die, I can come and celebrate forever with You in heaven. Yes, I'll come! I want others to know Jesus too. Lead them to me so I can tell them about Jesus and invite them to join in the celebration. Amen.

EVENING DEVOTION

Many are the sorrows of the sinful. But loving-kindness will be all around the man who trusts in the Lord.

PSALM 32:10

Those who trust in God are completely surrounded by His mercy—His caring, understanding, and forgiveness. This truth may be hard to grasp when life seems hard. And yet, whatever trouble you face, you have a layer of protection that can't be broken. Your life is completely in God's hands, and He will always and forever stay by your side.

DAY 40

AWESOME GIFT
(Psalm 33:1–3)

MORNING PRAYER

Heavenly Father, Psalm 33 says we should praise You with instruments and singing. So please make me an instrument in Your heavenly orchestra. Fill my heart with praise music. I will sing to You! Listen to Your people praise You. May our music dance with the stars and resonate with the waters of the deep, our praise filling every nook and cranny of space and time. Amen.

EVENING DEVOTION

Sing for joy in the Lord, you who are right with Him.
It is right for the pure in heart to praise Him.
PSALM 33:1

Why does God command that you worship Him? Is it because He has some arrogant need to be noticed and praised? That's not what it's about. If you were never to worship Him, your lack of praise would not affect Him in the least. But it would affect you. Praising God is good, refreshing, and life-giving for you. Don't neglect the wonderful gift of worshiping your God.

GOD ALONE
(Psalm 33:18–22)

MORNING PRAYER

Dear God, Your unfailing love gives me hope. Even when my hope fails, Your love doesn't. You watch over me. You help and shield me. Your unfailing love keeps me moving forward. If doubt creeps in, I will remember that You love me so much that You sent Jesus to save me from my sin. He is my greatest hope—in Him, I have the promise of life forever with You in heaven. Amen.

EVENING DEVOTION

No king is saved by the power of his strong army. A soldier is not saved by great strength. A horse cannot be trusted to win a battle. Its great strength cannot save anyone. . . . Our soul waits for the Lord. He is our help and our safe cover.
PSALM 33:16–17, 20

In what do you put your trust? Is it in popularity, material things, health, or your friends and family? Psalm 33 is a reminder that a feeling of completeness comes from God alone. Putting your trust in people and things is temporary. But putting your trust in God is forever. He is like a rock that will never move or crumble, unlike the things of this world.

EXODUS 32–33
MATTHEW 24:29–51
PSALM 34:1–7

HONOR GOD
(Matthew 24:42)

MORNING PRAYER

Heavenly Father, I'm hoping to start a career someday and possibly get married and have children. I know that when my life ends, You will bring me to meet You in heaven. You have that day planned already, along with all my days. I trust in Jesus as my Savior, and I promise I'll do my best to tell others about Him so they will be ready to meet You too. Amen.

EVENING DEVOTION

Give great honor to the Lord with me.
Let us praise His name together.
PSALM 34:3

No matter how much you achieve in this life, you will never be greater than God. It's far better to celebrate His greatness. It will draw you closer to Him. The bigger God is in your life, the more perspective you will have about how small and insignificant you are. When you see yourself as small, you will lean harder on Him, and leaning on God, in turn, will make you more powerful than you ever would be on your own. Surround yourself with others who celebrate and magnify God.

CHANGED

(Exodus 34)

MORNING PRAYER

You are the Lord! You are compassionate and gracious. You are slow to anger and abounding in love and faithfulness. You look for even the smallest sign of my faith. You love me unconditionally. And although You forgive sins, You are also fair. Jesus died for my sins so I can live forever! I didn't deserve that gift. Walk through life with me, Lord God. Keep me from heading in the wrong direction. Amen.

EVENING DEVOTION

*When Aaron and all the people of Israel saw
Moses, they saw that the skin of his face was
shining. They were afraid to come near him.*
EXODUS 34:30

Any encounter with God will certainly change you. The Israelites noticed that Moses' face shone brightly after he met with God. He had changed! When you commit to spending valuable time with God each day, you will be changed in a noticeable and powerful way too. No, your face won't literally shine, but God's glory will reflect off you and His love will work through you.

DAY 44

EXODUS 35:30–37:29
MATTHEW 25:14–30
PSALM 35:1–8

YOUR TALENTS
(Psalm 35:1–8)

MORNING PRAYER

Lord, when others seek to hurt me, You are my shield. Sometimes I feel like everyone is against me. That can suck the life out of me. So I run to You, asking You to shine Your light on me. Stand against anyone who tries to bring me down. Remind me that I'm worthy of love and respect. Thank You for saving me. I commit my life to You in return. Amen.

EVENING DEVOTION

The Lord has filled him with the Spirit of God, in wisdom, understanding, much learning, and in all work.
EXODUS 35:31

Our talents are God-given. So don't brag about your accomplishments. Instead, thank God for the skills He has given you. When you achieve something to be proud of, give God the credit. And don't take for granted the skills and talents He has given you. God wants you to use them with confidence to serve Him.

DOING GOOD
(Psalm 35:9–17)

MORNING PRAYER

Lord, You are so good to me. I have so much to be thankful for. Thank You for friends who stand up for me, who encourage me when I'm down, who praise You and celebrate with me when things are going well, who comfort me when I'm struggling. Thank You, God, for everything! The more I praise You, the less room I leave for worrying and complaining. Amen.

EVENING DEVOTION

"Then the King will say, 'For sure, I tell you, because you did it to one of the least of My brothers, you have done it to Me.'"
MATTHEW 25:40

Good deeds often go unnoticed and without thanks in this life. Maybe you wonder why you should bother going out of your way to help others. But even if the world doesn't notice, be confident that God notices. He sees all the instances in which you reach out to someone in need. God will reward you for your good works. In fact, in doing good for others, you will find yourself in a closer relationship with Him.

DAY 46

EXODUS 40
MATTHEW 26:1–35
PSALM 35:18–28

LEADER
(Matthew 26:6–13)

MORNING PRAYER

Lord, when I spend time alone with You in prayer, the rest of the world fades away. You are love, and I will love You back as much as I'm able. Fill me with Your Spirit, and I will worship You with praise. When I leave the privacy of my prayer time, I will carry Your love with me. Please help me to share it with others as I go about my day. Amen.

EVENING DEVOTION

When the cloud was lifted from the meeting tent, the people of Israel would go on their way through all their traveling days. But when the cloud was not lifted, they did not move on until the day when it was lifted.
EXODUS 40:36–37

In the desert, the Israelites had to rely on God for their next step. If the pillar of cloud moved, they moved. If it stayed in place, they waited. Even today, we rely on God's guidance for each next step. While you may wish His presence was as obvious to you as it was to the Israelites, you have God's Spirit living in your heart to guide you. Watch for Him to lead you into the next step of your life.

THE MOST IMPORTANT THING

(Leviticus 2:11–13)

MORNING PRAYER

Dear God, search all the hidden places inside me and help me to grow more like You. Help me to reject sinful things. Show me Your will—what You want for me. When I pray, I want the time we spend together to be joyful, like the best celebration I can imagine. I want to take everything You give me—all the love, joy, and knowledge—and share it with the world. Amen.

EVENING DEVOTION

*"But this has happened as the early preachers
said in the Holy Writings it would happen." Then
all the followers left Him and ran away.*
MATTHEW 26:56

You may feel uncomfortable reading in the Bible about the time all of Jesus' disciples abandoned Him to a violent mob that would treat Him—the Son of God—terribly. But often we treat Jesus in the same way. We don't speak about Him around friends who aren't Christians. We give other things priority over Him. We continue to sin. The most important thing in life is the time you spend with Jesus. Make *Him* your first priority.

WANDERING FROM THE PATH
(Matthew 26:69–27:26)

MORNING PRAYER

Lord Jesus, on the night You were betrayed, You reached out to the two men who went the furthest in denying You: Peter and Judas. I'm like Peter sometimes. I wander from the path You want me to follow. Thank You for forgiving me and leading me back to You. I pray for all the others who lose their way. Correct their steps; lead them back to You just as You have led me. Amen.

EVENING DEVOTION

The head religious leaders took the money. They said, "It is against the Law to put this money in the house of God. This money has bought blood." They talked about what to do with the money. Then they decided to buy land to bury strangers in.
MATTHEW 27:6–7

The money Judas received for betraying Jesus was used to buy a field in which strangers would be buried. In His very loving way, God caused that hate money to be used for good, to provide a final resting place for those who otherwise would have had none. God can take even the worst of circumstances and turn them around for good.

UNIQUE LOVE
(Leviticus 6:1–7)

MORNING PRAYER

Dear Lord, thank You for always being ready to forgive my sins. I thank You for the reminder that my sin doesn't only hurt my relationship with You but can also hurt others. When that happens, You want me to apologize to them. Sometimes, offering an apology is really hard for me to do! But it's what You want. Please give me the words to say and the courage to approach anyone I have hurt. Amen.

EVENING DEVOTION

*About three o'clock Jesus cried with a loud voice,
"My God, My God, why have You left Me alone?"*
MATTHEW 27:46

On the cross, Jesus asked why God had left Him alone. God could have pointed to each of us and said, "It is for you that I left Jesus alone on the cross." Jesus loves us. We struggle to understand why He would agree to suffer for people like us who would so easily leave Him. Jesus was left alone on the cross so we never would be alone. We should always remember that. Worship Jesus today and tell Him thank You.

DAY 50

LEVITICUS 7:22–8:36
MATTHEW 27:51–66
PSALM 37:7–26

OBEDIENCE
(Leviticus 8)

MORNING PRAYER

Lord God, even now You are preparing me for the work You want me to do. You have given me all the gifts and talents I need to do the work. So here I am, reporting for duty! Give me a clean heart so I can hear Your instructions clearly. Fill me with all the skills I need. I ask that everything I do will bring honor to You. Amen.

EVENING DEVOTION

The steps of a good man are led by the Lord. And He is happy in his way. When he falls, he will not be thrown down, because the Lord holds his hand.
PSALM 37:23–24

God orders your steps, and He is delighted to see you walking in His way. When you understand that God is with you every step of the way, you can experience His peace. And even when you stumble, you will not fall because Almighty God is by your side to catch you and hold you up.

SHARING YOUR FAITH
(Psalm 37:27–40)

MORNING PRAYER

Lord, I thank You for Christian friends who set a good example of living in ways to please You. Teach me as I watch them. Maybe they will learn from me too. Then we'll build each other up and help each other not to do things that displease You. Guide me to choose friends who know and love You. When we're together, help us to show the world that we belong to You. Amen.

EVENING DEVOTION

Jesus came and said to them, "All power has been given to Me in heaven and on earth. Go and make followers of all the nations. Baptize them in the name of the Father and of the Son and of the Holy Spirit. Teach them to do all the things I have told you. And I am with you always, even to the end of the world."
MATTHEW 28:18–20

Jesus wants you to be like one of His disciples and tell others about Him. When you know Him and accept Him as your Savior, He encourages you to share with others that if they accept Him too, they can join you in eternal life in heaven some-day. He has power over everything on earth, and He will give you the courage and power to tell others about His sacrifice on the cross. He has already taken care of the hard part.

DAY 52

LEVITICUS 11–12
MARK 1:1–28
PSALM 38

WHERE IS YOUR HOPE?

(Psalm 38)

MORNING PRAYER

Dear Lord, You know me. You know my strengths and weaknesses, what I hope for, and what things on earth steal my hope. You always do what's best for me at just the right time. Give me hope when I feel hopeless. Line up what I want with what You want for me. I pray, knowing You will help me. I trust You to answer me. Amen.

EVENING DEVOTION

For I hope in You, O Lord. You will answer, O Lord my God.
PSALM 38:15

Do you have the same confidence as David wrote about in Psalm 38—that God will hear when you call to Him? Where is your hope? If your hope is in your own abilities or achievements, then you will find yourself disappointed. Attach your hope to God's love and care for you, and you will never be let down.

PRAYER FOR THE SICK
(Leviticus 13)

MORNING PRAYER

Dear God, I thank You for Your concern for the sick. Today I pray for those who have physical problems. Open my eyes to understand their pain. Give me a loving heart to pray for them. Lead me to help however I can. I pray for the necessary support they need, for their health, for their daily activities, and I pray that You would bless them with caring friends. Amen.

EVENING DEVOTION

"O Lord, let me know my end and how many days I have to live. Let me know that I do not have long to stay here."
PSALM 39:4

You are planning a long and happy life. But sometimes it's important to think about how short life really is. In God's eyes, it's just a matter of time before you meet Him in heaven. How would your life change right now if you knew when your life would end? You don't need to worry about dying. You have the hope of heaven in your heart. For now, do what pleases God and lead others to do the same.

OUTCASTS
(Mark 1:40–45)

MORNING PRAYER

Lord Jesus, You have done so many good things for me and the people I love. Help me to spread the good news of Your power and love to everyone I meet. I want to be like the man You healed from a skin disease—He just couldn't help himself and talked about You everywhere. You are worthy of all my praise, Jesus. Thank You, and amen.

EVENING DEVOTION

Jesus put His hand on him with loving-pity. He said, "I want to. Be healed."
MARK 1:41

Notice the difference in today's Old and New Testament readings. Leviticus shows us how a leper was treated and what was needed for him to be healed. Mark shows us a different time and the change that came with Jesus. He was willing to touch even the most contagious people. Jesus brought in a new time when no one was an outcast. He welcomes everyone, no matter who they are. Even if they are filled with sin, Jesus is able to heal them.

FAMILY
(Mark 3:13–34)

MORNING PRAYER

Lord Jesus, I thank You for my family, for placing me with people who pray and dream for me. How grateful I am that You have put other Christians all around me to serve as examples. When You created Adam, You knew he shouldn't be alone. So You created a companion for him. Thank You, Lord, that I'm not alone in the world. I have my family, my friends, and most of all *You*! Amen.

EVENING DEVOTION

Jesus ate in Levi's house. Many men who gather taxes and others who were sinners came and sat down with Jesus and His followers. There were many following Him.
MARK 2:15

Isn't it amazing that Jesus preferred hanging out with sinners and outcasts rather than showing others how popular He was? Jesus didn't care about being popular, and neither should you. If you ever find yourself becoming too concerned about your social image, just remember what Jesus did and try to be more like Him.

DAY 56

LEVITICUS 16–17
MARK 4:1–20
PSALM 41:1–4

FREEDOM!
(Leviticus 16:1–3)

MORNING PRAYER

Dear God, sometimes when I pray, I feel like I'm a little boy, just hanging out with his dad. I'm free to tell You anything without being afraid. You are my heavenly Father, and I am Your son. You love me! I am amazed by how big, powerful, and wise You are. I can come to You day and night and know You will be there to listen to and help me. Amen.

EVENING DEVOTION

*For on this day your sin will be taken away
and you will be clean. You will be made free
from all your sins before the Lord.*
LEVITICUS 16:30

In Bible times, one day a year, the high priest would make an offering to ask God to forgive all the people for their sins. Back then, the offering would cover only the sins of one year. But when Jesus died for our sins on the cross, His offering of Himself changed everything. His dying for our sins meant God will forgive our sins now and forever.

CALM
(Mark 4:21–23)

MORNING PRAYER

Lord Jesus, sometimes I'm afraid to tell others about You. Other times I feel I don't have the right words. Then I hear Your voice in my heart: *"By yourself you have nothing. With Me you have everything you need. Let your light shine."* Jesus, forgive me when I hide my light—when I don't tell others about You. Help me never be afraid to share everything I know about You. Amen.

EVENING DEVOTION

He got up and spoke sharp words to the wind. He said to the sea, "Be quiet! Be still." At once the wind stopped blowing. There were no more waves.
MARK 4:39

The same God who controls the wind and the sea lives inside your heart today. Fear has no place and no power against Almighty God. When the waves of life are threatening to take you under, remember who reigns as King in your heart. Ask Him to still the fear in your life and give you a sense of peace.

DAY 58

LEVITICUS 20
MARK 5
PSALM 42–43

HEALING
(Mark 5:34)

MORNING PRAYER

God, where are You? When I pray, I don't always hear Your voice. The door between us seems to be closed. But still, I put all my hope in You. I feel Your love, I know You're with me. Night and day, I will continue to pray and sing praises to You. Lord, even when I don't hear You, I know You are there. My Savior, my God, You will never leave me. Amen.

EVENING DEVOTION

He said to her, "Daughter, your faith has healed you.
Go in peace and be free from your sickness."
MARK 5:34

Jesus changed the life of the woman in Mark 5 in more ways than one. First, He healed her bleeding. More importantly, He called her "daughter." This woman would have been an outcast in her society, with little human contact because of her condition. So can you imagine how she must have felt when Jesus called her His daughter—a term of endearment and belonging? Similarly, you are called a son of God and forever belong to Him, no matter what happens.

ALMIGHTY GOD

(Psalm 44)

MORNING PRAYER

Dear Lord, thank You for surrounding me with adults who know You and live to serve You. Help me to grow in faith by looking to them as my role models. Mold me to be like them. Even better, mold me to be more like You. One day, I want people who are my age now to look at me as their role model, a wise man of God. Amen.

EVENING DEVOTION

"Do not sin against My holy name. I will be honored among the people of Israel. I am the Lord Who makes you holy. I brought you out of the land of Egypt to be your God. I am the Lord."
LEVITICUS 22:32–33

Often in Leviticus, God says, "I am the Lord." The Israelites had no better reason to follow His law than He was their God. He was the supreme ruler, the Creator of the universe. He is the same for us today. God does not change. He is and always will be the one true Lord, ruler of us all. That's why we set our hearts to obey Him and follow Him wherever He leads.

DAY 60

LEVITICUS 23–24
MARK 6:14–29
PSALM 45:1–5

CELEBRATE
(Leviticus 23)

MORNING PRAYER

Creator God, I thank You for holidays and special days, for the gift of time and seasons. Thank You for celebrations. Thank You that every day I can praise You because it is a day You made! Even in the silliness of National Roller Coaster Day, I thank You. Every day, I will look for something special You have hidden within the day just for me, and I will praise You. Amen.

EVENING DEVOTION

"Work may be done for six days. But the seventh day is the Day of Rest, a holy meeting when you do no work at all. It is the Day of Rest to the Lord in all your homes."
LEVITICUS 23:3

The laws in Leviticus sometimes seem harsh, but God put them in place for the good of His people. God made the Sabbath a day of rest because He knew that for our well-being, we need to have a day to rest and recharge. Do you honor this rest that God has given you? Do your best to keep the Sabbath a day when you rest and honor Him.

REST IN GOD
(Mark 6:39–44)

MORNING PRAYER

Jesus, I've often felt alone in a group of thirty. I can't imagine being in a group of five thousand strangers. Did Your disciples feel outnumbered in that crowd? I might feel alone sometimes, but You are always with me, knowing what I need even before I ask. Have I missed Your miracles while I struggled on my own, searching for answers? Whatever I'm looking for, God, You have just what I need. Amen.

EVENING DEVOTION

He said to them, "Come away from the people. Be by yourselves and rest." There were many people coming and going. They had had no time even to eat.

MARK 6:31

If you feel guilty about taking time to rest in a world that demands so much action, remember that Jesus encouraged His disciples to rest from the work they were doing for Him. Make time every night to rest in God. He is like a charging station, giving you power for your next day's work. Tomorrow, go back out into the world refreshed and ready for school, work, and play.

ACTIONS
(Leviticus 26)

MORNING PRAYER

God, You know me better than I do. You know my past, my struggles in the present, and my dreams for the future. You live inside my heart, and You want me to focus on You. Help me to listen to Your words and to obey You. I never want to shut You out or avoid You. That would be the greatest mistake of all. I can't do life on my own. I need You. Amen.

EVENING DEVOTION

He said to them, "Isaiah told about you who pretend to be someone you are not. Isaiah wrote, 'These people honor Me with their lips, but their hearts are far from Me.'"
MARK 7:6

Are you the kind of person of whom God might say, "He honors Me with his lips, but his heart is far from Me"? Ask God for your heart to be so filled with love for Him that it overflows into praise and service for His kingdom. Do your best to please Him so your actions prove these words to be true: "God, I honor You with my lips, and my heart belongs to You."

BE STILL
(Psalm 46:10)

MORNING PRAYER

Father God, the greatest thing in all my life is knowing You. I want to spend more time with You, but I have trouble keeping still. Teach me the patience of silence so I might hear You more clearly. When I speak, teach me to be quiet and listen before I open my mouth. When I answer others, I want them to hear Your voice, not mine. I want my words to honor You. Amen.

EVENING DEVOTION

Be quiet and know that I am God. I will be honored among the nations. I will be honored in the earth. The Lord of All is with us. The God of Jacob is our strong place.
PSALM 46:10–11

Psalm 46 is one of the best psalms to read if you need some comfort. Even if your whole world seems to be coming apart at the seams, you have no reason to be afraid because God is with you. He will never leave you. Be still. Read and meditate on the words of Psalm 46. Know that God is in complete control and that He is the one in whom you will find both strength and rest in times of trouble.

JOY!
(Psalm 47)

MORNING PRAYER

Lord, David's psalm makes me want to stand up and shout, to sing and dance before You. I want to join hands with people around the world and praise You. The skies would echo with the sound of clapping hands and joyful cries from all nations. That's the world I want to see, united in praise of You and not divided! I thank You that one day that will be the reality. Amen.

EVENING DEVOTION

*Show your happiness, all peoples! Call
out to God with the voice of joy!*
PSALM 47:1

Like the people in Psalm 47, you can shout with joy to God. Why? Because He always wins against sin. He rules the world. It might seem like things on earth are a mess and people aren't getting along, but God is sitting on His throne in heaven directing everything that happens. God rules the earth, so shout for joy that He is your God, perfect and good in every way.

I BELIEVE!
(Numbers 3:13)

MORNING PRAYER

God, You gave Your firstborn Son—Your only Son—to save me from my sin. If I get married and have children someday, I will give them to You. I will ask You to lead and guide them throughout their lives. And whatever You decide is the right path for them to follow, I will follow Your guidance to help them be their best. Everything I have belongs to You, God. I love You. Amen.

EVENING DEVOTION

At once the father cried out. He said with tears in his eyes, "Lord, I have faith. Help my weak faith to be stronger!"
MARK 9:24

Notice in Mark 9 how Jesus didn't heal the man's son right away. Instead, He waited until the man was entirely sure that he totally needed Jesus. He even needed help to believe. Don't be ashamed to ask God to help you believe in His love and power. It's when you reach rock bottom that He lovingly draws you closer to Him. When you recognize how small you are, you realize just how big God is.

FOREVER AND EVER
(Mark 10:13–16)

MORNING PRAYER

Lord, some people say that since baby animals are cute, it makes them less likely to be attacked. Was that Your plan? I'd like to think so. All babies are cute. You have the well-being of all children in mind even before they are born. You have planned every day of their lives. Lord, I want to help children younger than me. I want to lead them to know You. Will You help me, please? Amen.

EVENING DEVOTION

*This is God, our God forever and ever. He
will show us the way until death.*
PSALM 48:14

Serving a God who has lived on earth as a human is such an encouragement. Jesus experienced suffering and loss, just as we do. He died and then came back from death as Savior and Lord. There's nowhere you can go and nothing you can do that Jesus won't be able to guide you through. He totally understands you. You don't even have to be afraid of dying one day. On that day, Jesus will take your hand and walk you into heaven. He is your God forever and ever.

CHANGING LIVES
(Mark 10:46–52)

MORNING PRAYER

Lord Jesus, like Bartimaeus, I want to see—more of You, more in Your Word, more of Your majesty all around me. I want eyes to view other people as You do. I want X-ray vision that uncovers the sin hidden deep in my heart. I want a clear view ahead to see the path You've laid out for me. I want to see You wherever I go and in everything I do. Amen.

EVENING DEVOTION

"Whoever wants to be first among you, must be the one who is owned and cares for all. For the Son of Man did not come to be cared for. He came to care for others. He came to give His life so that many could be bought by His blood and be made free from sin."
MARK 10:44–45

Instead of the triumphant earthly king the Jews expected, Jesus—the Messiah—came as a lowly servant who would end up dying to save us. Instead of raising up an army of courageous men, King Jesus chose followers who would humbly serve others. His kingdom is one in which weakness is used to a greater advantage than strength. Look to Jesus as your example. His ways can change lives and move mountains.

CHRIST IS LORD
(Numbers 6:24–26)

MORNING PRAYER

Dear God, Numbers 6:24–26 is a powerful blessing for others. I'm going to make it my prayer this morning and put it in my own words: Lord, bring good to my family and friends. Shine Your love on them and be kind to them. Please show Your favor toward them and give them peace. Bless my family and friends today and every day. Amen.

EVENING DEVOTION

Like sheep they are meant for the grave. Death will be their shepherd. And those who are right with God will rule over them in the morning. Their bodies will be eaten by the grave, so that they have no place to stay. But God will free my soul from the power of the grave. For He will take me to Himself.
PSALM 49:14–15

Those who don't believe in Jesus' gift of salvation will always be searching for more in life. They always want more stuff, thinking it will bring them joy. They are looking to fill up that empty space in their hearts, the place reserved for Jesus. But life is different for those who know Jesus. They understand that life isn't about stuff. Jesus fills their hearts so full that they have no need for earthly treasures. The gift of His presence and the promise of eternal life in heaven are their true treasure.

RELATIONSHIP
(Psalm 50:1–15)

MORNING PRAYER

Dear God, You want me to call on You. It's all about relationship. You want me to call on You when I'm in trouble so You can rescue me. Then I will give You thanks and honor You. Most important, You want me to listen to Your words. You want to speak to me uninterrupted. Please open my ears, God. Teach me to listen more than I speak. Amen.

EVENING DEVOTION

If I were hungry, I would not tell you. For the world is Mine, and all that is in it. . . . Give a gift of thanks on the altar to God. And pay your promises to the Most High.
PSALM 50:12, 14

Your relationship with God can be hard to understand because it's like no other relationship you have. There's nothing you can offer God that He can't get on His own. He owns the world—the universe! So many of our earthly relationships are based on what we can give and get. We like to be needed. But with God, we have to set aside the desire to be needed and concentrate on what we can give Him without worrying about what we might receive in return. He wants you to give Him your all.

DAY 70

NUMBERS 8:5–9:23
MARK 12:28–44
PSALM 50:16–23

FOLLOW HIM
(Mark 12:41–44)

MORNING PRAYER

Lord Jesus, sometimes I'm ashamed of how little I have given You. The woman in today's reading gave everything she had to You, but I may struggle to give even a little. Open my heart, open my hands, to give freely with joy. Teach me to be willing to give until it's no longer easy or convenient. Teach me to give up something I want but don't need. Teach me to be generous. Amen.

EVENING DEVOTION

Sometimes the cloud stayed from evening until morning. When the cloud lifted in the morning, they would leave. If the cloud stayed during the day and the night, when it was lifted, they would leave that place. Even when the cloud stayed over the meeting tent for two days, or a month, or a year the people of Israel would stay in that place and not leave. They would leave when it was lifted.

NUMBERS 9:21–22

The Israelites had to live day by day, watching and waiting for the cloud of God's presence to move. Once the presence of God moved, they had to follow it without delay. Are you as willing to pack up your life and your comforts to follow God wherever He wants you to go? That is what He asks of you—to follow Him. Be careful not to get so attached to the things and places of this world that you hesitate to follow God wherever He leads.

WEIGHT OF SIN
(Numbers 10:35–36)

MORNING PRAYER

Lord God, as I start this new day, I already know You are going on ahead of me. Chase my enemies away. Help me to hold my head high and walk with confidence. Tonight, when I come to bed to pray and rest, stand guard over me while I sleep. I pray this prayer for all Your people in this world. Go ahead of us today and guide us through. Amen.

EVENING DEVOTION

I have sinned against You, and You only. I have done what is sinful in Your eyes. You are always right when You speak, and fair when You judge.

PSALM 51:4

David understood that every sin is an insult to God and hurts Him deeply. We often imagine that our sins are pretty much harmless. But Jesus didn't die for something that didn't matter. He didn't die for what is harmless. It's important to recognize that every sin hurts God. Only when we realize how much our sin hurts Him can we truly come to appreciate the sacrifice Jesus made.

HUMILITY
(Psalm 51:10–19)

MORNING PRAYER

"Create in me a pure heart, O God" (Psalm 51:10 NIV). That was David's prayer. Lord, forgive me for the times I've sinned. Help me to do better. I thank You for Jesus, that He died for me so I can have a clean heart. I'm not worthy of You, God. But Jesus makes me right in Your eyes. Help me to see sin when I meet it and to reject it. Amen.

EVENING DEVOTION

*Now Moses was a man with no pride, more
so than any man on the earth.*
NUMBERS 12:3

Numbers 12:3 says no one on earth had less pride than Moses. The opposite of *prideful* is *humble*. Moses was not full of himself. At first, this statement may seem surprising. Moses was, after all, the leader of the Israelites. But rather than making him arrogant, the fact that he had seen and spoken with God was the very thing that made him humble. The more we know God and see how small we are compared to His greatness, the more humble we become.

MILK AND HONEY
(Psalm 52:8–9)

MORNING PRAYER

God, if people put me down, remind me that I belong to You. Nothing they say or do can hurt me. I'm like that olive tree in Your garden. You will never uproot me and throw me away. I trust in Your love. For all You have done, are doing, and will do for me, I praise You. Let those who make fun of me look more deeply at me and see You and Your goodness. Amen.

EVENING DEVOTION

*If the Lord is pleased with us, then He will
bring us into this land and give it to us. It is a
land which flows with milk and honey.*
NUMBERS 14:8

Joshua and Caleb had remarkable courage and faith. They believed in the power and faithfulness of God despite their enemies and their faithless, complaining friends. It would have been easy for them to follow popular opinion and side with the crowd. But they had enough faith in God to speak up against the majority. How often do you shy away from speaking up for your beliefs because you are scared? Fortunately, our faithlessness does not affect God's faithfulness.

FOOLS?

(Mark 14:32–36)

MORNING PRAYER

Lord Jesus, when I come to You feeling sad, You understand what I'm going through. The sadness You felt when Your disciples left You must have been overwhelming. You knew You were about to die. You pleaded with God, asking if there was another way for humankind to be saved. Yes, You know what it feels like to be sad. Remind me of this truth when my heart hurts. You get it, and You love me. Amen.

EVENING DEVOTION

The fool has said in his heart, "There is no God." They are sinful and have done bad things. There is no one who does good.
PSALM 53:1

Psalm 53:1 says that those who believe there is no God are fools. All of creation points to the existence of God. So don't ever think you are a fool for believing in God and doing your best to please Him. He sent Jesus so you can live forever in heaven. Those who don't believe are the fools. Pray that their eyes are opened to see that God not only exists but also has a wonderful plan for their lives.

ULTIMATE EXAMPLE

(Numbers 16)

MORNING PRAYER

Lord, sometimes my preferred candidate loses, and I ask You why. The people of Israel asked You why, too, when they had to accept a leader they didn't want. God, remind me that You are the supreme leader. Nothing happens that You don't already know about. Everything falls into place as part of Your plan. Help me to accept results I don't like, and remind me to trust in You. Amen.

EVENING DEVOTION

*The head religious leaders and the teachers of the
Law made fun of Him also. They said to each other,
"He saved others but He cannot save Himself."*
MARK 15:31

God doesn't often use flashy, eye-catching techniques to accomplish His will. Jesus could have come down off the cross or called angels to shock the crowd. But God had another plan. Instead of saving Himself, Jesus suffered shame, insults, and utter humiliation to become an ultimate example for us. Sometimes God asks us to put up with things we don't like. Often His plan is outside our ability to understand. We just need to trust that His will for us is good.

IMPACT
(Mark 15:40–41)

MORNING PRAYER

Lord Jesus, I'm in awe of Mary Magdalene, Joseph of Arimathea, and all the other people who were near the cross. I thank You for their example. I thank You for Christian people who are my heroes. I ask that my faith be like theirs—strong, confident, and able to get through hard times. They stood up for You even when doing so wasn't popular. Help me to learn from their example. Amen.

EVENING DEVOTION

Joseph, who was from the city of Arimathea, was an important man in the court. He was looking for the holy nation of God. Without being afraid, he went to Pilate and asked for the body of Jesus.
MARK 15:43

Joseph of Arimathea was bold enough to stand in support of Jesus when he came to take the Lord's body for burial. When most of Jesus' disciples were hiding, Joseph publicly honored Jesus. This was a risky move on his part. He easily could have been sent away from his homeland or worse. But the impact Jesus had on him was great enough to overcome his fear. Would you be as bold as Joseph of Arimathea to align yourself with someone who was just killed by a hateful mob?

PRECIOUS
(Numbers 20:12)

MORNING PRAYER

Heavenly Father, I can't imagine how Moses felt when You said he wouldn't enter the promised land. He must have been disappointed. Still, he had to accept Your will—You were his God, and You never make mistakes. I learned from Moses that when I face disappointment, I need to trust in Your perfect plan. I might not get what I want now, but You have something even better waiting for me in the future. Amen.

EVENING DEVOTION

It was early on the first day of the week when Jesus was raised from the dead. Mary Magdalene saw Him first. He had put seven demons out of her.
MARK 16:9

Even when He arose from the dead, Jesus showed the world His heart for ordinary people. The first person He appeared to was not someone popular or important in those days but rather a woman. In the culture of that time, women were not highly valued. But this woman loved Jesus enough to be the first one at the grave very early in the morning. The hearts of those who love Jesus are much more valuable to Him than a person's social standing on earth.

DAY 78

NUMBERS 21:1–22:20
LUKE 1:1–25
PSALM 56:8–13

GOD IS FOR YOU
(Psalm 56:8–13)

MORNING PRAYER

Dear God, I thank You, but not just when everything goes well. Although I do give thanks for good times, I give You thanks this morning for the times when I stumble and You lift me up. I'm alive today, and I thank You. I trust in You for everything, especially when things don't go my way. You are my God, and You are always good to me. Amen.

EVENING DEVOTION

*Then those who hate me will turn back when
I call. I know that God is for me.*
PSALM 56:9

Do you believe God is for you, or do you believe He only likes you when you do what He wants? Believing that God is for you means unshakable confidence that everything happening in your life is designed by Him for your good and His glory. That's hard to believe when things don't go well. But God *is* for you! One day, you'll be able to look back and see the powerful plan He had for your life where everything worked together for good.

NOT ALWAYS
WHAT IT SEEMS
(Luke 1:46–56)

MORNING PRAYER

God my Savior, You love me, a teen guy, just as You loved Mary, the teen girl. She recognized all You had done for her, and she praised You with great joy. I praise You with great joy too! Compared with You, I am nothing. But You are so good to me all the time. Maybe, like Mary, I'll be a parent someday. If so, I hope my children, and my grandchildren, and all my descendants will know and love You forever. Amen.

EVENING DEVOTION

"But the donkey saw me and turned from me these three times. If she had not turned from me, for sure I would have killed you, and let her live."
NUMBERS 22:33

You never know what frustrating thing in your life is actually God's way of saving you from harm. In Balaam's story (Numbers 22), he was angry with his donkey for turning away from the path. You can understand Balaam's anger as things just wouldn't go his way. But the angel of the Lord told Balaam that the very thing he was angry about was what saved his life. Think about it: a frustrating situation in your life might just be God protecting you.

DAY 80

HISTORY
(Numbers 24)

MORNING PRAYER

Dear Lord, sometimes the prayers You put in my heart aren't the ones I expect. Like when You want me to ask You to bless the people who hurt me. Lord, praying for my enemies is hard, but I know it's Your will. Help me to pray for their blessing. Show me how to love them despite my anger and hurt. Amen.

EVENING DEVOTION

Her first son was born. She put cloth around Him and laid Him in a place where cattle are fed. There was no room for them in the place where people stay for the night.
LUKE 2:7

Jesus was born into a world that apparently had no room for Him, forcing Him to be born in a stable. Shepherds, ordinary men, were the first to enter His birthplace and see His face. It's doubtful any of us would have written the story of the most important birth in history this way. But that's the awesome beauty of it all. The birth of Christ is not a man-made story; it is the story of the Creator and Savior of the world.

MARVELOUS BLESSING

(Numbers 27:1–11)

MORNING PRAYER

Dear Lord, I'm thankful that You love me just as I am. You never look at me and say, "He's not good enough!" I'm always handsome in Your sight. I'm Your son, a son of the King. You created me. You sent Jesus to save me from my sin. I pray that one day I will live as a prince in Your kingdom, surrounded by Your love and carrying out kingdom duties. Amen.

EVENING DEVOTION

*"Lord, now let me die in peace, as You have said.
My eyes have seen the One Who will save men from
the punishment of their sins. You have made Him
ready in the sight of all nations. He will be a light
to shine on the people who are not Jews. He will be
the shining-greatness of Your people the Jews."*
LUKE 2:29–32

God gave His servant, Simeon, a marvelous blessing by allowing him to see Jesus before he died. Simeon understood the prophecies, the Old Testament teachings about a Savior, and he recognized Jesus for who He was—Savior to Israel, the Gentiles, and the world. How special that he could see the Savior who would soon bring into reality all the promises of God that Simeon knew and held on to as his hope.

REASON TO PRAISE
(Numbers 27:15–21)

MORNING PRAYER

Heavenly Father, Moses spent a lifetime focusing his thoughts and prayers on others. Even as he was dying, he thought about and prayed for the people of Israel. I want to be like Moses—someone who genuinely cares. I want to spend my life finding needs and trying to meet them. Every day, I want to pray for my family, my friends, and even people I don't know. Lord, help me to pray. Amen.

EVENING DEVOTION

But as for me, I will sing of Your strength. Yes, I will sing with joy of Your loving-kindness in the morning. For You have been a strong and safe place for me in times of trouble.
PSALM 59:16

How often do you openly praise God for His power, compassion, and forgiveness? He leads us through every day of our lives, yet we sometimes fail to acknowledge His guidance. We often struggle to praise Him privately in our own hearts for all He has done for us, let alone tell others how wonderful He is. No matter what happens in your life, you still have many reasons to praise God at the end of the day.

FULLY MAN, FULLY GOD
(Luke 3:21–22)

MORNING PRAYER

Jesus, what did You say at Your baptism? You didn't have any sins to confess. Did You ask for Your Father's blessing and strength? Thank You for allowing us to see and hear part of that prayer, when God spoke for human ears to hear and the Holy Spirit came on You like a dove. I pray that my time with You will help to make others see You in me. Amen.

EVENING DEVOTION

Cainan was the son of Enos. Enos was the son of Seth. Seth was the son of Adam. Adam was the son of God.
LUKE 3:38

What an amazing mystery it is that Jesus was both fully man and fully God when He came to earth. He had human ancestors. He came from relatives from whom He would have inherited strengths, weaknesses, and physical traits. When God chose to come to earth to live among us, He didn't show up with a fancy entrance or with others proclaiming He was God. Instead, He chose to come as part of a family.

DAY 84

NUMBERS 31
LUKE 4
PSALM 60:6–12

TROUBLES
(Psalm 60:6–12)

MORNING PRAYER

Lord, You are so great! I love being in Your family. You call me Your own. You know what I need before I even ask. I can always come to You with confidence, asking for help. Remind me of that when I try to do something for myself that only You can provide. I want my Christian family to grow. Help me find friends who know and love You. Amen.

EVENING DEVOTION

O give us help against those who hate us. For the help of man is worth nothing. With God's help we will do well. And He will break under His feet those who fight against us.
PSALM 60:11–12

Where do you turn first when you are struggling with something? Have you ever had the experience in which you realized hours after anxiously working through a problem that you still hadn't asked the Lord for help? In this psalm, we're told that our only completely trustworthy source of help is our heavenly Father. While He can (and does) use the people around us to give us sound wisdom and advice, we still should always turn to Him with our troubles before going to anyone else.

AWARE

(Psalm 61:2–4)

MORNING PRAYER

Dear God, sometimes I feel like I'm under so much pressure. I get overwhelmed with things to do and anxious thoughts swirling around in my head. I need peace. You have been my comfort in the past, and I need You to comfort me again. Protect me from hurt. Keep me safe. Lighten my load. Calm me down. I want to rest in You, safe and sheltered under Your powerful wings. Amen.

EVENING DEVOTION

When Simon Peter saw it, he got down at the feet of Jesus. He said, "Go away from me, Lord, because I am a sinful man."
LUKE 5:8

Peter truly understood his standing before God. In Luke 5:8, he is so aware of his sinfulness and Jesus' holiness that he asks Jesus to leave him. What would you have done if you were Peter? Are you aware of how messy your sins are, or do you generally think you have your behavior under control and your act pretty well together?

DAY 86

NUMBERS 34–36
LUKE 5:17–32
PSALM 62:1–6

SOLID
(Psalm 62)

MORNING PRAYER

Heavenly Father, when I can't sleep or when I'm worried, You are there for me. My hope comes from You. I want to wake up each morning feeling refreshed and ready. Today, I will rely on You for strength. I will trust in Your protection. If things get tough, I will remember that I can always find shelter under Your wings. Amen.

EVENING DEVOTION

He alone is my rock and the One Who saves me.
He is my strong place. I will not be shaken.
PSALM 62:6

David understood that with God as his safe place, he could not be moved. He called God his rock. The Hebrew word used here wouldn't have meant a stone or even a boulder but rather a mountain. Just as mountains are unshakably solid, so is God for those who seek shelter in Him. Run to the Rock and hide yourself in His shadow.

FEAR OR FAITH?

(Luke 6:1–10)

MORNING PRAYER

Father, sometimes I create trouble for myself by getting stuck in my way of doing things. Doing what I want has even taken away the joy of others around me. Forgive me, Lord. Help me to loosen up a little and change my ways so my actions and words are more aligned with Your will. Guide me through reading the Bible to change my behavior and become more like You. Amen.

EVENING DEVOTION

"But even so, you did not trust the Lord your God, Who goes before you on your way. He finds a place for you to set up your tents. He uses fire to show you the way to go during the night. During the day He uses a cloud to lead you."
DEUTERONOMY 1:32–33

Moses scolded the people for not believing God about the land He had promised them. This was the God who had stayed with them for the entire journey, showing them the way in a cloud by day and as their light by night. This was the God who had proven Himself over and over again. And yet the Israelites chose fear instead of faith. Is your first reaction to a difficult situation fear or faith? Hasn't God proven Himself to you as well?

FOR THE GLORY OF GOD
(Psalm 63:1–5)

MORNING PRAYER

Lord, You are my God. I want to see You. I catch glimpses of You when I read the Bible, but all of You is beyond the eyes of my imagination. Your greatness makes me choose to praise You with my words, to praise You today and every day, to lift up my hands and sing to You. God, You are my life and my reason for living. Amen.

EVENING DEVOTION

He looked at His followers and said, "Those of you who are poor are happy, because the holy nation of God is yours."
LUKE 6:20

Earthly success isn't spiritual success. In His sermon, Jesus called those who are poor, hungry, weeping, and hated by others blessed—hardly words we would use to describe a successful life. If someone doesn't fit into our definition of earthly success, it does not in any way mean that God is not blessing that person. So much can be learned from Jesus' followers who use their poverty, hunger, sorrow, and mistreatment for the glory of God.

100 PERCENT SUCCESS

(Deuteronomy 4:29–31)

MORNING PRAYER

Heavenly Father, You are not just God; You are *my* God, and You always treat me with care. You are my God, always faithful to me, never breaking Your promises to me when I misbehave. You even use the bad stuff in my life to guide me back to You. Every minute of my life unfolds in Your sight. Teach me to follow You even more. I want to give You my all. Amen.

EVENING DEVOTION

"But from there you will look for the Lord your God. And you will find Him if you look for Him with all your heart and soul."
DEUTERONOMY 4:29

God is not a God who makes Himself hard to find. He does not try to hide from us so we can't know Him. In times when God seems far off or seems to have abandoned you, maybe you haven't been seeking Him as much as you need to. He promises to be found by those who seek Him—so look for Him in the Bible and everywhere around you. You have a 100 percent chance of finding Him.

DAY 90

DEEP LOVE
(Luke 7:11–17)

MORNING PRAYER

Lord Jesus, I love You and trust You. I thank You for the gift of my family. When I'm troubled and I think things will never get better, my family is there to help me. Even better, Lord, You are there. And You can do anything! Nothing can get in my way. Nothing is greater than You and Your ability to work miracles. You are my help and my Savior. Amen.

EVENING DEVOTION

When they came near the city gate, a dead man was being carried out. He was the only son of a woman whose husband had died. Many people of the city were with her. When the Lord saw her, He had loving-pity for her and said, "Do not cry."
LUKE 7:12–13

Jesus was all about compassion. His actions were inspired by a deep-seated love for people, even people He didn't know. Pray that God will put in your heart the same kind of compassion Jesus so wonderfully displayed. In today's passage, Jesus changed this woman's life, but even a small act of compassion and kindness has the power to turn a life around.

YOUR GUIDE
(Deuteronomy 8:4)

MORNING PRAYER

Dear God, every morning is like putting on clean clothes. You provide me with everything I need for the day. You clothe me in protection from head to toe. Whatever the weather—if today is good or if it comes with trouble—I will be dressed and ready. Your love surrounds me and guides me. You are with me wherever I go. Thank You, God, for preparing me for my day. Amen.

EVENING DEVOTION

"You will remember all the way the Lord your God led you in the desert these forty years, so you would not have pride, and how He tested you to know what was in your heart to see if you would obey His Laws or not."
DEUTERONOMY 8:2

Moses told the Israelites to remember their trying journey through the wilderness—to remember the humbling times, the proving grounds, and the heavy-duty struggles. They were to remember that God was leading them through those times every step of the way. It is good to spend time remembering the paths God has led you down. Remember how faithfully He has led you so you can step boldly into the future, trusting Him as your guide.

DAY 92

DEUTERONOMY 10–11
LUKE 7:36–8:3
PSALM 65:1–8

THE HEART
(Luke 7:36–43)

MORNING PRAYER

Dear Lord, I confess that sometimes I'm more like the Pharisees than the sinful woman in this story. I judge people and think their sin is worse than mine. Forgive me. Open my eyes to see and accept everyone as my equal. We all are sinners, and we all are Your children. We live with and learn from each other. Help me to remember that. Amen.

EVENING DEVOTION

The proud religious law-keeper who had asked Jesus to eat with him saw this. He said to himself, "If this Man were One Who speaks for God, He would know who and what kind of a woman put her hands on Him. She is a sinner."
LUKE 7:39

In Luke 7:39, the Pharisee was criticizing Jesus for not knowing that the woman who was showing Him such honor was a sinner. Meanwhile, Jesus not only knew exactly what this woman had done in the past and the shame that was now in her heart but also recognized the disrespectful thoughts the Pharisee was thinking. The Pharisee had grossly underestimated the insight and power of the Man he had invited to dinner.

BEAUTIFUL CREATION
(Deuteronomy 13:1–4)

MORNING PRAYER

God, would I be any more prepared for Your tests if I knew about them ahead of time? Instead, they show up when I least expect them, like a pop quiz. I pray that I won't listen to people who offer to help me cheat or try to get me to sin. I pray that I won't be led astray by lies or false information. Help me to listen to You, God, and obey. Amen.

EVENING DEVOTION

The fields of the desert are filled with water. And the hills dress themselves with joy. The grass lands are covered with birds. And the valleys are covered with grain. They call out for joy and sing.
PSALM 65:12–13

Have you ever been outside on one of those days when you can almost hear nature praising its Maker? Have you ever seen a sight so incredibly powerful that you have to start praising God as well? What a wonderful gift that God has so blessed us with by putting His beauty and creativity on full display for our pleasure. We should never take His creation for granted.

DAY 94

DEUTERONOMY 14:1–16:8
LUKE 8:22–39
PSALM 66:1–7

WHERE IS YOUR FAITH?

(Luke 8:22–25)

MORNING PRAYER

Jesus, sometimes I feel like those disciples in the boat. It seems like You're asleep, not paying any attention to the storm raging around me. Forgive me for my lack of faith, for not coming to You before a situation reaches a crisis stage. I thank You that You are "in the boat" with me all the time. I will reach out to You in trust, believing You will keep me safe and at peace. Amen.

EVENING DEVOTION

He said to them, "Where is your faith?" The followers were surprised and afraid. They said to each other, "What kind of a man is He? He speaks to the wind and the waves and they obey Him."
LUKE 8:25

Are you ever surprised when God does something amazing in your life? The disciples in today's passage were in complete awe when Jesus calmed the wind and the waves. Jesus scolded them, asking them, "Where is your faith?" Why is it that we are sometimes surprised when we see God's goodness in our lives? Is our faith so weak that we doubt His power and love?

ORDINARY
(Luke 8:50)

MORNING PRAYER

Heavenly Father, I need to learn to believe in You more than in what You will do. I know You can do anything. You can perform miracles. But sometimes I don't get what I expect or want from You. Those are the times I have to remember that Your thoughts and plans are greater than my own. You always give me what is best, even when I can't understand. I praise You, Lord. Amen.

EVENING DEVOTION

Her spirit came back and she got up at once.
Jesus told them to bring her food.
LUKE 8:55

Today's passage in Luke is a great example of how God uses both miracles and ordinary things to complete His work. Jesus miraculously healed the girl, but then He told her parents to give her something to eat. This instruction seems so ordinary after He just performed the great miracle of bringing their daughter back from the dead. We shouldn't be surprised when God uses ordinary means to carry out His plans.

DAY 96

DEUTERONOMY 19:1–21:9
LUKE 9:1–22
PSALM 66:16–20

THE NEXT STEP
(Deuteronomy 20:5–9)

MORNING PRAYER

God, too often I struggle with finding the right balance. At times I shut myself off from others, preferring to do my own thing. Other times I stay so busy with friends and activities that I neglect what's important. Too much of one thing. Too little of another. I need to learn to manage my time. I pray this morning, asking for Your wisdom to guide me as I schedule my days. Amen.

EVENING DEVOTION

"He will say to them, 'Hear, O Israel. Today you are going into battle against those who hate you. Do not let your hearts become weak. Do not be afraid and shake in fear before them. For the Lord your God is the One Who goes with you. He will fight for you against those who hate you. And He will save you.'"
DEUTERONOMY 20:3–4

You aren't facing enemy armies like the Israelites did, but you still have battles to fight nearly every day. Some may be more difficult than others, but at some point we all need courage to face the next step in life. Go into each new day with confidence, knowing God is the one who fights for you. Don't be afraid. The all-powerful God is on your side.

BLESSED BY HIM

(Psalm 67:1–2)

MORNING PRAYER

Dear God, this morning I pray that You will bless me and shine Your goodness on me. And when You bless me, show Yourself to everyone on earth. Let them see Your goodness so they want it for themselves. Lead my friends, my family—everyone—to You so they too can have the promise of eternal life in heaven. Amen.

EVENING DEVOTION

May God show loving-kindness toward us and bring good to us. May He make His face shine upon us. May Your way be known on the earth, and Your saving power among all nations.
PSALM 67:1–2

We all want God to bless us. But why? In today's psalm, the author asked to be blessed so others might know of God's greatness. Use the blessings God has given you as a starting point to tell others about how great He is. Always be willing to speak of God and all He has done for you so others may be blessed by Him as well.

DEUTERONOMY 23:9–25:19
LUKE 9:43–62
PSALM 68:1–6

YOU BELONG
(Luke 9:57–62)

MORNING PRAYER

Lord, sometimes I'm afraid that I've valued Your good gifts more than I have You, the giver. Forgive me. When You ask me to let go of something I want or love, instead of saying, "Yes, Lord," sometimes I say, "Wait a minute!" I'm sorry. I don't always understand how You work, but I want to give You all honor and glory, all the time, no matter what. Amen.

EVENING DEVOTION

God in His holy house is a father to those who have no father. And He keeps the women safe whose husbands have died. God makes a home for those who are alone. He leads men out of prison into happiness and well-being. But those who fight against Him live in an empty desert.
PSALM 68:5–6

It's no wonder God feels so strongly for children without parents, people who are alone, and those who feel like they don't belong. His heart for these people is seen throughout the entire Bible. He is the Father to those who have none and the protector of the lonely. He places those without a home into families. If you are ever lonely or feel like you don't belong, remember that God is always by your side as your loving Father.

THINK ABOUT THIS

(Deuteronomy 26:12–15)

MORNING PRAYER

Lord God, everything I am and have belongs to You. Thank You for all Your gifts. Teach me to share what You have given me. I want to obey all Your commands, and I want to remember to worship You all day, every day. Forgive me when I don't remember all You have done for me when I'm not willing to share, and when I fall short of Your expectations. Amen.

EVENING DEVOTION

"Even so, you should not be happy because the demons obey you but be happy because your names are written in heaven."
LUKE 10:20

More than anything on earth, Jesus wants us to celebrate that our names are written in God's book. Every day, more names are added as people accept Jesus as their Savior. We should always be grateful for what God gives us, and we should be happy when we accept His gifts. But there is no greater gift or reason for celebrating than knowing you'll have eternal life with Him in heaven.

DEUTERONOMY 28:15–68
LUKE 10:21–37
PSALM 68:15–19

TOO MANY BLESSINGS?

(Luke 10:21)

MORNING PRAYER

Lord Jesus, forgive me when I come to You like a know-it-all, thinking I only need to ask Your opinion to compare it to mine. I want to accept Your ways as best—all the time. I know that everything You give me is good. Fill me with Your joy! Open my eyes to the wonder of all that is You. In return, I will praise You. Thank You, Jesus. Thank You for all Your blessings. Amen.

EVENING DEVOTION

*Honor and thanks be to the Lord, Who carries our
heavy loads day by day. He is the God Who saves us.*
PSALM 68:19

The Lord carries our heavy loads day by day. What a great mental image He presents in Psalm 68:19. The blessings God gives us each day are almost too many to carry. Our lives overflow with God's goodness. Take a few minutes to think about that and write down some of the blessings God has given you this week.

CHOICES
(Deuteronomy 29:2-6)

MORNING PRAYER

Lord, forgive me for ever taking You for granted. As I go about my day, bring to mind the things You've done for me. As I read stories in the Bible, remind me of the many ways You have blessed Your people. I have no right to what You give me. Everything comes *from* and belongs *to* You. Help me to remember that. Every blessing is a gift. Amen.

EVENING DEVOTION

"I call heaven and earth to speak against you today. I have put in front of you life and death, the good and the curse. So choose life so you and your children after you may live."
DEUTERONOMY 30:19

Just like the Israelites, we are faced with a choice each day: Will we choose sin and its consequences, or will we choose life and a blessing? The choice seems simple enough—as Moses said, choose life. It's easy to slip into doing our own thing instead of keeping our eyes on God and what He wants though. Think about ways you can spend more time with Him every day. Do your best to live to please Him. Then wait for the ways He will bless you.

DEUTERONOMY 31:1–32:22
LUKE 11:24–36
PSALM 68:28–35

GOD WILL NEVER
LEAVE YOU

(Psalm 68:28–35)

MORNING PRAYER

God, I pray for everyone on earth, especially those who don't know You. I want them to choose You as their God and Savior so they can have eternal life in heaven. I want them to give their all to You and give You power over their lives. Please lead them to You today. Make this a day when many decide to enter Your kingdom. Please save them, Lord. Give them a new life. Amen.

EVENING DEVOTION

*"Be strong and have strength of heart. Do not be
afraid or shake with fear because of them. For the
Lord your God is the One Who goes with you. He will
be faithful to you. He will not leave you alone."*

DEUTERONOMY 31:6

Before Moses died, he encouraged the Israelites to be courageous because God would go with them and would never fail or leave them. God will never fail you or leave you either. How do you know it's true? Because He left His own Son so He would never have to leave you. No one can be trusted more fully than God, who turned away the one He loved so you could enter heaven someday. God will never leave you alone.

SAVE ME!
(Psalm 69:1–9)

DEUTERONOMY 32:23–33:29
LUKE 11:37–54
PSALM 69:1–9

MORNING PRAYER

Dear God, some days I just want to shout to You, "Save me!" Things have a way of piling up and becoming too much. When that happens, sometimes I forget I can rely on You. I try to do it all myself until. . .I can't do it anymore. Forgive me for relying on myself instead of You. You have always been my help before. So, God, save me from myself because I need *You*. Amen.

EVENING DEVOTION

Save me, O God, for the waters have almost taken my life.
PSALM 69:1

The Bible is filled with stories of people we can relate to—imperfect people in need of God. Psalm 69 is just one such example of a person crying out to God for help. Many times in the Bible, you will see people realizing just how much they need God and crying out to Him. Don't ever be afraid or ashamed to say, "God, save me!" You are no different from the people in the Bible. God is your helper. You need Him.

NOTHING TO FEAR

(Joshua 1:1–9)

MORNING PRAYER

God, what a difference between Joshua and Moses. Moses kept asking You to send someone else, but Joshua went right to work. Make me more like Joshua than Moses, at least when it comes to what You've called me to do. Help me to see Your will for me today as clearly as You helped Joshua. And remind me of Your words: *"Don't be afraid. I'm with you wherever you go."* Amen.

EVENING DEVOTION

*"I say to you, My friends, do not be afraid of those
who kill the body and then can do no more. I will
tell you the one to be afraid of. Be afraid of Him
Who has power to put you into hell after He has
killed you. Yes, I say to you, be afraid of Him!"*
LUKE 12:4–5

In Luke 12:4–5, Jesus offers some strong words. But His words are actually comforting. You have nothing to be afraid of! If you trust in Jesus as your Savior, you are a son of God. People can't really hurt you, and God will never hurt you. You have God's promise that on the day you die, you will be with Him in heaven. How you get there is a mystery. But *where* is for certain. Heaven is your home.

PROMISE KEEPER

(Luke 12:32–34)

MORNING PRAYER

God, You say You want to give me Your holy nation. Does that mean You want to give me heaven? I don't have to do anything to earn my ticket into Your holy place except to believe in Jesus, but, God, I want to do my best here on earth to show You my gratitude. Let me live each day remembering that You already have given me everything in my future home with You. Amen.

EVENING DEVOTION

Then Joshua said to the people, "Make yourselves holy. For tomorrow the Lord will do powerful works among you."
JOSHUA 3:5

Joshua's faith shines brightly in this verse. He didn't tell the people to live holy lives just in case God decided to do something amazing. He didn't tell the people to hope and pray that God would show up. No! He told them to live holy lives because God *would* do wonders the next day. There is no doubting or second-guessing. Joshua knew his God. He knew Him to be an absolutely faithful promise keeper.

DAY 106

JOSHUA 5:13–7:26
LUKE 12:41–48
PSALM 69:29–36

DON'T WAIT
(Joshua 7:1–12)

MORNING PRAYER

Forgive me, Lord, for when I grab something that belongs to You and bury it deep, saving it for myself. Forgive me for my selfishness. Forgive me for those times when I take the credit for what You have done for me. Remind me that sometimes when things go well, I slip into trusting in myself instead of in You. Correct my steps so I follow Your commands. Amen.

EVENING DEVOTION

"That servant is happy who is doing his work when the owner comes."

Luke 12:43

Do you live every day expecting Jesus to come back soon, or do you put off serving Him thinking you will have more time in the future? You are young, but your time on earth in God's eyes is short. Do your best each day to serve Him. Tell others about Jesus; share His story. Treat others in the ways Jesus would treat them. Don't wait for another, better time. Live today expecting Jesus to show up any minute.

RESISTANCE
(Luke 12:57)

MORNING PRAYER

Lord, sometimes I doubt myself and my ability to serve You. Remind me that any good that comes from my actions or words really comes from You. It's not whether I'm prepared but whether I trust You to do what You've promised. I trust You to guide me. If I head down the wrong path, stop me. Show me when I should ask for advice and when I should trust You without asking questions. Amen.

EVENING DEVOTION

"Do you think I came to bring peace on the earth? I tell you, no! I came to divide."
LUKE 12:51

Jesus told His disciples that He came not to bring peace but to divide. Not exactly a heartwarming idea. But it can be encouraging for you if friends turn against you simply because you follow Jesus. Jesus said that others would push against Him and anyone who followed Him. When people turn against you for following Jesus, it can be a sign that you are doing exactly what Jesus wants—following Him faithfully.

DAY 108

JOSHUA 10:1–11:15
LUKE 13:1–21
PSALM 71:1–6

MORE HOPE
(Psalm 71:1–6)

MORNING PRAYER

Lord, You are my hope. Thank You for leading me. Thank You for the strength that hope gives me with each twist and turn in my life. I'm looking forward to completing projects and starting new things. I can't wait to follow You and see where You lead me. I wonder about the future. I imagine. I dream. But my hope rests in You. Amen.

EVENING DEVOTION

For You are my hope, O Lord God. You are my trust since I was young.
PSALM 71:5

Where is your hope found? In school? Family? Your things? Your popularity? In today's psalm, the author wrote that his hope is set firmly in the Lord. When you hope and trust in God, you won't be disappointed. This doesn't mean that hoping in God is a way to avoid trouble. Instead, in hard times, God will prove you can trust Him so you can learn to hope in Him even more.

HOPE ALWAYS

(Psalm 71:7–16)

MORNING PRAYER

Dear God, I'll always have hope. My hope is based on trying to emulate Your character and Your faithfulness. You never fail those who trust in You, and I'll do my best not to fail those who trust in me. I will tell them about all the wonderful things You do and about Jesus' promise of heaven. Help me, Lord, to be more like You and to give hope to others. Amen.

EVENING DEVOTION

*But as for me, I will always have hope and
I will praise You more and more.*

PSALM 71:14

The hopefulness of those who truly know God is amazing. We see examples of it all through the Bible in God's prophets, disciples, and followers. In today's passage, we see it in David. His life situation doesn't sound like anything to be happy about—even his enemies thought God had left him. Nonetheless, David continued to hope in God, praise Him, and speak of His goodness. Only God can give this kind of strength and hopefulness to His children.

COMFORT ALL AROUND

(Joshua 14:6–15)

MORNING PRAYER

Heavenly Father, I admire the older Christians in my life. Those who are my grandparents' age inspire me. Although they might not be as strong physically as they were in their younger days, they are still super strong in their faith. They've conquered the mountains that got in their way, and they've grown in wisdom and faith. God, when I get older, I want to be like them, still moving forward with strength and my eyes set on You. Amen.

EVENING DEVOTION

You have shown me many troubles of all kinds. But You will make me strong again. And You will bring me up again from deep in the earth. Add to my greatness, and turn to comfort me.

PSALM 71:20–21

At times, God may bring you through trouble, but you can be as confident as David was in this psalm that God will raise you up again to where things are better. David used the powerful imagery of God comforting him on every side—God's comfort surrounds and protects His people. Even in (and often *especially* in) the darkest moments, you can feel His comfort and strength holding you up.

WORTHY
(Luke 14:27)

MORNING PRAYER

Father, You say I can't be Your disciple if I don't pick up my cross. What does that mean? What might You ask me to do or give up? Following You comes with a price tag—obeying what You ask of me, and what You might ask scares me sometimes. I don't want to look into the future afraid. I know You love me, God. Make me unafraid to follow You. Amen.

EVENING DEVOTION

*"In the same way, whoever does not give up
all that he has, cannot be My follower."*
Luke 14:33

Are you worthy to be Jesus' disciple? It's something to think about. Jesus said only those willing to give up everything they have can be His disciples. He's not asking you to give away everything you have all at once. But would you be willing to if He did ask? To grow in faith means working toward the point when you would give up everything for Jesus. What might you do to grow your faith one day at a time?

DAY 112

JOSHUA 19:17–21:42
LUKE 15:1–10
PSALM 72:1–11

ADOPTED
(Joshua 20)

MORNING PRAYER

Lord, I pray that You will help everyone who has been falsely accused of doing something wrong. I pray for my country to provide safety and to be welcoming to people from around the world who seek freedom and fair judgment. You are the fairest judge of all. I believe You judge now just as You did in Bible times. Please save those who are mistreated and falsely accused. Amen.

EVENING DEVOTION

"I tell you, it is the same way among the angels of God. If one sinner is sorry for his sins and turns from them, the angels are very happy."
Luke 15:10

When someone accepts Jesus as Savior, it is no small thing in heaven. In fact, Jesus said that the angels rejoice when someone prays to receive Him. Think about that. On the day you welcomed Jesus into your heart, angels shouted a resounding, "Hallelujah!" You were adopted into God's family and became a valuable part of His kingdom—and that's worth celebrating!

GOOD THINGS
(Luke 15:11–32)

MORNING PRAYER

Heavenly Father, sometimes when I read Jesus' parable about the prodigal son, I see myself. Sometimes I leave You and go my own way. But when I come back, You welcome me. And You don't just welcome me—You celebrate my return! Correct me whenever I feel like leaving You. Transform my attitude of complaining and wanting more to one of gratitude. Open my eyes to Your amazing love that never changes. Amen.

EVENING DEVOTION

*Every good promise which the Lord had made
to the people of Israel came true.*
JOSHUA 21:45

All of God's promises will come true. No good gift from Him will fail. God promises us good things because He loves us in a way that we can't even begin to understand. His love is entirely unselfish. Think about this: He gave up His only Son, whom He loved so much, so that you could have eternal life with Him in heaven. Hold on to God's promises. He loves you and He will always be faithful to you.

BE FAITHFUL
(Joshua 24)

MORNING PRAYER

Lord God, I thank You for the people who came before me and said, "We will serve the Lord." I thank You for those in my life right now who stand with me and say, "We will serve the Lord together." Lead me to serve You faithfully every day of my life. And if I have children and grandchildren someday, help me teach them to serve You too. Amen.

EVENING DEVOTION

"If you have not been faithful with riches of this world, who will trust you with true riches?"
LUKE 16:11

Today's passage in Luke is an excellent reminder that we need to be faithful in every part of our lives. That means honoring God in everything you do. Honor Him in the ways you treat others. Honor Him by doing your best in school and by giving your all when you compete in sports or do chores at home. Be faithful in the little things, and then God will know He can trust you with bigger things.

IN GOD'S PRESENCE
(Judges 2:1–3)

MORNING PRAYER

Lord, the words of Judges 2:1–3 remind me that there are consequences for my actions. When I disobey You, I sometimes suffer the result and it's not pleasant. Like any good father, You want me to follow Your rules. If I don't, I can make trouble for myself. That's on me for not doing what You wanted. But I'm grateful that when I mess up, I can ask Your forgiveness and You will always forgive me. Amen.

EVENING DEVOTION

*Until I went into the holy place of God.
Then I understood their end.*

PSALM 73:17

In the first part of Psalm 73, the writer began to doubt whether following God was worthwhile. He became so worked up that his thoughts were too painful to even consider. But the turning point of the psalm comes in verse 17: "until I went into the holy place of God." When you are anxious and overwhelmed, run to God. Don't neglect your time with Him. Being in His presence can transform your feelings of anxiety and doubt.

GRACE
(Luke 17:11–17)

MORNING PRAYER

Jesus, thank You for showing me grace—all the goodness and kindness I don't deserve. Even when I mess up badly, You extend Your grace to me. Too often I take for granted all that You give me. I sin again and again, each time hoping that next time I'll do better. With grace, You love me just as I am, all the time. Grow my faith in You. Make me forever grateful for Your grace. Amen.

EVENING DEVOTION

One of them turned back when he saw he was healed. He thanked God with a loud voice. He got down on his face at the feet of Jesus and thanked Him. He was from the country of Samaria.
LUKE 17:15–16

Why did one of the men that Jesus healed return? He returned because he knew how sick he had been, and he knew that Jesus alone was responsible for his healing. When the leper was sick and rejected by those who were afraid of catching his disease, Jesus showed him grace. Are you aware of what your life would be like without His grace? Imagine yourself as the sick man in today's reading. Would you return to Jesus to praise and thank Him for His loving-kindness?

FILLED UP
(Luke 18:1–8)

MORNING PRAYER

God, sometimes when I pray I wonder why the answer doesn't come right away. But then it does, in the blink of an eye, in such a way that only You could have done it. When the answer comes that way, I'm sure it comes from You, and I give You all the credit. Thank You for filling me up with Your answers and with everything else that is You. Amen.

EVENING DEVOTION

"But the man who gathered taxes stood a long way off. He would not even lift his eyes to heaven. But he hit himself on his chest and said, 'God, have pity on me! I am a sinner!'"
Luke 18:13

The man in today's reading understood who he was compared to God. He was totally unworthy to be in the presence of a perfectly holy God, so he stood humbly before God and asked for mercy. By following this man's humble behavior, we become more powerful than we can imagine. When we kneel before God, knowing we have nothing to offer in our weakness, He fills us up with His strength.

THROUGH GOD
(Judges 6:36–40)

MORNING PRAYER

Lord, when You call me to do something unexpected, I know it's okay to ask for confirmation—to know that You are really the one leading me. Every day, I have faith in You. But when a really big and life-changing opportunity arises, I want to be sure I am following You, not someone else or my own will. When I ask, "Is it really You, God?" please be quick to answer. Amen.

EVENING DEVOTION

The Lord said to Gideon, "The people with you are too many for Me to give Midian into their hands. Israel might say with pride, 'Our own power has saved us.'"
JUDGES 7:2

God knew He had to make Gideon's army small and weak for them to understand that the victory came only from Him. He didn't want the soldiers puffed up with pride, thinking they had done it themselves. When things go well, be careful to give God the credit. It is when you think you can accomplish something great all by yourself that God might put a roadblock in your way as a reminder that you are successful because of Him and Him alone.

SAVING POWER OF JESUS
(Psalm 74:12–17)

MORNING PRAYER

Dear God, forgive me when I create mini gods—myself, family and friends, celebrities, people, and things I admire. You are the one and only God, ruler of the earth. You are the Savior of the world and my Creator. You said I should have no other gods but You. Please open my eyes to the other gods in my life and help me to get rid of them. Amen.

EVENING DEVOTION

*Zaccheus stood up and said to the Lord, "Lord,
see! Half of what I own I will give to poor people.
And if I have taken money from anyone in a wrong
way, I will pay him back four times as much."*

LUKE 19:8

Zaccheus was a selfish criminal—a tax collector who stole from people. He hurt many families to satisfy his own comfort and wants. But his heart and lifestyle changed when Jesus called him out and went to his house. Don't ever imagine that a self-absorbed and cruel person is past the saving power of Jesus. He came to earth to save especially the worst of sinners. He continues on that mission today.

DAY 120

JUDGES 9:24–10:18
LUKE 19:29–48
PSALM 74:18–23

LITTLE DETAILS
(Psalm 74:18–23)

MORNING PRAYER

Dear Lord, this morning I pray for the needs of others, those who are defenseless and those who need healing. I pray for those who have been put down and need confidence in themselves again. I ask You to comfort those who are sad. I pray for those who choose sin over You, and I ask that You would save them, Lord, with the promise of eternal life in heaven. Amen.

EVENING DEVOTION

Those who were sent found everything as Jesus had told them.
LUKE 19:32

The Gospel writers Matthew, Mark, and Luke told the story of the disciples finding a donkey right where Jesus told them it would be. It may seem like a little, unimportant thing to include in the stories of when Jesus walked the earth. But it is a great example of how God plans every detail of our lives. Even the tiniest details of your life matter to Him.

WORKING FOR GOD
(Luke 20:17–18)

MORNING PRAYER

Jesus, You are like a rock I can hang on to in a windstorm. I can trust in You and depend on You. I know if I hang on tightly to You, I will be okay. But if I stop trusting You and let go, I will get into trouble. Even then, Jesus, You would help me. I thank You that I can always count on You, even if, for a while, I lose my faith. Amen.

EVENING DEVOTION

*For honor does not come from the east or the west
or from the desert. But God is the One Who decides.
He puts down one and brings respect to another.*
PSALM 75:6–7

God is the one who sees our good work and trusts us to do even more for Him. He might also let us know when we aren't working hard enough to help with His plans here on earth. Whatever kind of work you do—at home, school, or wherever—work as if you are working for God. He is the one who sees you doing a good job, and He will reward you.

SERVING
(Luke 20:34–38)

MORNING PRAYER

Dear God, I wonder sometimes what heaven is like. I'm sure it is wonderful. But for now, I'm living here on earth and my mission is to serve You. Teach me to serve You well. Help me to grow in wisdom. I want to live today and every day with my mind set on doing what is good and right. I praise You, God, my teacher, and my friend. Amen.

EVENING DEVOTION

"Look out for the teachers of the Law. They like to walk around in long coats. They like to have people speak words of respect to them in the center of town where people gather. They like the important seats in the places of worship. They like the important places at big suppers."
LUKE 20:46

What are your reasons for doing good? Do you want people to recognize your good work and praise you, or are you working for God and giving Him the praise? You can expect God to bless you when you work for Him. When you do a good job and people say, "Good for you!" you can answer with something like, "I couldn't have done it without God." Make sure others know that all good things come from Him.

VALUABLE OFFERING
(Judges 15:18; 16:28)

MORNING PRAYER

Dear God, sometimes my prayers are selfish, like those of Samson when he was young. Other times they are more like the older Samson—focused on You and what *You* want. Help me to grow in the way I pray. I don't just want to pray for You to fulfill my wants; instead, I want to pray for You to show me what I need. I want my prayers to be like music to Your ears. Amen.

EVENING DEVOTION

He said, "I tell you the truth, this poor woman has put in more than all of them. For they have put in a little of the money they had no need for. She is very poor and has put in all she had. She has put in what she needed for her own living."
LUKE 21:3-4

Have you put working for God on hold because you felt you didn't have enough to offer? The poor widow in today's passage gave an offering that by the world's standards was worthless. But by God's standards, it was the most valuable offering she could have given. God doesn't measure a person's value the way the world does. So offer Him your time and talents—all those things you're good at. Nothing is too small. Whatever you have to offer Him is enough.

WORDS OF HOPE
(Luke 21:33)

MORNING PRAYER

Father God, forever is hard to imagine. I live in a world where time matters. Forever is endless. The Bible says You are forever. You are with me right now and our relationship is forever. Nothing can destroy it. Your Word, the Bible, is my forever right here on earth. It gives me hope and teaches me to prepare for life in heaven with You. I will read and grow from it every day. Amen.

EVENING DEVOTION

*"Heaven and earth will pass away, but
My Words will not pass away."*
LUKE 21:33

You can't know for sure what will happen tomorrow. But God's Word gives you all the hope you need that a good future lies ahead. If the world were to end tomorrow, you have hope that God wouldn't end with it. He wouldn't leave you alone. He would pick you up with His strong arms and take you to be with Him. It's His promise to you, and God always and forever fulfills every one of His promises.

REMEMBER HIS WONDERS
(Psalm 77:1–11)

MORNING PRAYER

Lord God, sometimes I come to You in prayer feeling angry or sad. I say to You, "God, are You listening?" And then I hear Your voice answer in my heart, *"Which is more important: for Me to listen to you—or for you to listen to Me?"* Forgive me for thinking prayer is all about me. You listen whenever I pray. Remind me to listen to You. Amen.

EVENING DEVOTION

Has God forgotten to be loving and kind? Has He in anger taken away His loving-pity? . . . I will remember the things the Lord has done. Yes, I will remember the powerful works of long ago.
PSALM 77:9, 11

We've all been in situations that make us question whether God is as good as He says He is. When things aren't going your way, don't turn away from Him. Instead, think about all the good things He has already done for you. Turn to God and trust in Him. It's possible that the very thing causing you trouble today is something you will look back on with fond memories of God's goodness as He helped you through.

JUDGES 20:24–21:25
LUKE 22:31–54
PSALM 77:12–20

PERFECT PLAN
(Luke 22:39–46)

MORNING PRAYER

Lord Jesus, prepare me to fight back when I'm faced with a choice to do what is wrong. Every day, I feel pressure to follow my friends and do something that would displease You. Please help me to be strong. Remind me of Your instructions in the Bible, and help me obey them. If I mess up, Jesus, please forgive me. I'm not perfect, but I promise I'll try to do my best. Amen.

EVENING DEVOTION

He said, "Father, if it can be done, take away what must happen to Me. Even so, not what I want, but what You want."
LUKE 22:42

"Not what I want, but what You want." This is a difficult attitude to have, even in little, everyday struggles. We have no problem following God's will when it lines up perfectly with ours. But as soon as God's plan is different from our own, doubt begins to creep in. We wonder if our way isn't best after all. When this happens, pray. Ask God to help you get back on the path that leads to what He wants for you.

NEVER TOO WEAK
(Ruth 1:16–17)

MORNING PRAYER

Lord God, I thank You for the people in the Bible, for showing me their real problems and their acts of faith. Ruth was an amazing person. If You lead me someplace different, I pray You will make me strong like Ruth. Lead me every step of the way. Help me to accept the tasks You give me, no matter how great or small. Amen.

EVENING DEVOTION

*But Peter said, "Sir, I do not know what you are saying."
And at once, while he was talking, a rooster crowed.
The Lord turned and looked at Peter. He remembered
the Lord had said, "Before a rooster crows, you
will say three times that you do not know Me."*
LUKE 22:60–61

Have you ever denied knowing the Lord? If a classmate asked, "Are you a Christian?" would you proudly answer, "Yes," or would you dance around the question? Even Peter, who loved Jesus and promised to stand by Him, failed. Filled with fear, Peter denied knowing Jesus. Our God is so good that even when we deny and disappoint Him time and time again, He will forgive us and continue to love us. You are never so weak that He'll to deny His love for you.

GOD'S PEOPLE
(Luke 23:32–46)

MORNING PRAYER

Lord Jesus, some of Your last words on the cross were a prayer. You asked for forgiveness for those who killed you. I wonder, would I have been able to pray that prayer? Even now, I sometimes struggle to forgive those who hurt me. You rose from the dead to give me life. I want to be a reflection of You, forgiving others and leading them to know You. Please help me, Lord, to be more like You. Amen.

EVENING DEVOTION

The neighbor women gave him a name. They said, "A son has been born to Naomi!" And they called him Obed. He is the father of Jesse, the father of David.
RUTH 4:17

You can live anywhere in the world and be one of God's people. Christians live everywhere, all over the world. How much do you know about your ancestors? Were they Christians? Maybe you are the first in your family to know Jesus. Whether you come from a long line of Christians or you're the first, you can help add more people to God's kingdom. Always be ready to tell others about Jesus and His promise of eternal life.

SELFLESS
(1 Samuel 1)

MORNING PRAYER

Dear Lord, I wonder if I could be like Hannah and give my child back to You. What an unselfish thing to do. But then I remember that You did the same thing for us. You gave up Your Son, Jesus, so we can have a better life—eternal life—in heaven. Lord, help me to be unselfish. Everything I have is Yours. Amen.

EVENING DEVOTION

But Hannah did not go. For she said to her husband, "I will not go up until the child no longer needs to be nursed. Then I will bring him before the Lord, to stay there forever."
1 Samuel 1:22

Hannah understood that Samuel was a gift from God. She had begged for a child, and then when God granted her wish, she decided to give Samuel back to God to serve Him in the tabernacle. How awesome! We often hold so tightly to God's gifts that we forget where those gifts came from in the first place. Hannah was so grateful to God that she unselfishly gave back the best gift she had ever received and returned her son to the Lord.

1 SAMUEL 2:22–4:22
JOHN 1:1–28
PSALM 78:17–24

REASON FOR LIFE

(John 1:9–13)

MORNING PRAYER

Lord Jesus, when I welcomed You into my heart, You "adopted" me and gave me rights to everything You have. You gave me a new heart—one filled with Your love. I am Your son, and You are my Father forever. God, I pray that You will give all those who don't believe in You a new heart—a heart that welcomes You in to stay forever. Amen.

EVENING DEVOTION

The Word (Christ) was in the beginning. The Word was with God. The Word was God. . . . Christ became human flesh and lived among us. We saw His shining-greatness. This greatness is given only to a much-loved Son from His Father. He was full of loving-favor and truth.
JOHN 1:1, 14

In the days when the Bible was written and John wrote this passage, the Greek word that became "Word" in our English Bibles meant "the reason for life." John says the reason for life—the "Word"—is Jesus. God sent Jesus to us in human form to live with us on earth. Then, after He died, Jesus became our reason for life. Through Him we have the gift of forever life in heaven.

NO MATCH FOR GOD
(Psalm 78:25–33)

MORNING PRAYER

God, sometimes I'm like the Israelites. When I sin and You correct me, I try to ignore You. I close myself off from You and keep on sinning. When I do that, I know I'm heading in the wrong direction. You are so good to me. You bless me in so many ways. God, I want to continue to receive those blessings. Teach me to say no to sin and yes to obeying You. Amen.

EVENING DEVOTION

But when they got up early the next morning, they saw that Dagon had fallen on his face to the ground in front of the special box of the Lord. And Dagon's head and both his hands were cut off and lying in the doorway. Only the body of Dagon was left.
1 SAMUEL 5:4

The story at the start of 1 Samuel 5 is almost funny, as time and time again the city's idol is found on its face in front of the ark of God. But what isn't funny is the truth in this story: no other god is a match for our God. No idol can stand up to the power of God. All will come crashing down at His feet. Are there any idols in your life—sports? video games? money? girls?—anything you have made more important than God?

1 SAMUEL 8:1–9:26
JOHN 2
PSALM 78:34–41

THE MOST UNLIKELY
(Psalm 78:34–41)

MORNING PRAYER

Heavenly Father, living for You takes faith. It's hard sometimes to believe in what I can't see. Forgive me when I doubt You. I'm still amazed that I—just a little speck of sand on earth, unlikely to matter—am so important to and loved by You. I thank You for Your blessings. Thank You for correcting me when I'm wrong, for forgiving me, and for always leading me back to You. Amen.

EVENING DEVOTION

Saul answered, "Am I not a Benjamite, from the smallest of the family groups of Israel? Is not my family the least important of all the families of Benjamin? Why then do you speak to me this way?"

1 SAMUEL 9:21

Saul couldn't believe God would appoint him king. He was from the smallest tribe and the most unimportant family in Israel. Clearly, God must have made a mistake. Little did Saul know that choosing the most unlikely is what God often does. He uses the weak, the small, or those who feel unimportant, leading them to do His work. Since power comes only from Him, God doesn't need to choose strong, powerful, or important people to accomplish His will.

THE LIGHT
(John 3:1–22)

MORNING PRAYER

Lord Jesus, I like how Nicodemus acted based on what he knew: You were a teacher, a man sent from God to do miracles. I wish more people would act on what little they know of You. I'd like to be more like Nicodemus. Open my eyes to see You. Open my heart to learn from You. Be the light for my path and my teacher all the days of my life. Amen.

EVENING DEVOTION

"The Light has come into the world. And the Light is the test by which men are guilty or not. People love darkness more than the Light because the things they do are sinful. Everyone who sins hates the Light. He stays away from the Light because his sin would be found out."
JOHN 3:19–20

Don't be surprised if people make fun of you because you believe in Jesus. People made fun of Jesus too. It's sad that so many choose to live without Jesus lighting their way. Their lives can get pretty dark sometimes. The Bible says Jesus is the light of the world. It's your job to shine His light into the darkest corners of the world by encouraging others (even if just a few) to come to believe in Jesus and love Him.

GOD'S REMINDER
(1 Samuel 12:20–25)

MORNING PRAYER

Lord God, Samuel made praying for Israel his life's work. You've placed me in a circle of family and friends. I'm part of a community. I pray for those close to me, but there are others I forget to pray for. Open my eyes to those around me—even out of my sight—who need prayer. Then lead me to pray for them and to keep praying for them until You provide an answer. Amen.

EVENING DEVOTION

He allowed His people to be killed with the sword. And He was very angry with those who belong to Him.
PSALM 78:62

How could a loving God give His people over to nations that hated them? God wants so much for us to follow Him into eternal life that He goes to great lengths to make it happen. Sometimes He allows hard circumstances to remind us to turn to Him as the source of our strength. He provides everything that's good. For Him to allow you to fill up with sin would be far worse than any trial He leads you through.

SEEK AFTER GOD
(Psalm 78:67–68)

MORNING PRAYER

Dear God, You rejected Joseph and chose Judah. That might not have made sense to some people, but You never make wrong choices. You are always right. You have a plan for everything You do. When I see something that is unfair or unjust, help me to remember that You are in control. You are good to those who seek You, and You will make things right. Amen.

EVENING DEVOTION

*Jesus said, "My food is to do what God wants
Me to do and to finish His work."*
JOHN 4:34

Food is essential to life. Without it, we die. In John 4:34, Jesus said that His "food" was to do the will of His Father. Doing God's will was what kept Jesus going; it was His life's purpose. Is doing God's will as important to you as your daily food? You would notice if you went a day without food. Would you notice if you went a day without seeking God? Without Him, you'll starve yourself of all the goodness He wants to provide.

THE WAY YOU SEE THINGS

(1 Samuel 16:6–7)

MORNING PRAYER

Lord, this morning I want to do my best to look good. Thanks for the reminder that I don't have to look or be perfect to find acceptance with You. When You bring new people into my life, don't let me reject them due to appearance. Help me instead to see people as You do, as created and loved by You. Amen.

EVENING DEVOTION

When they had come, Samuel looked at Eliab and thought, "For sure he is the Lord's chosen one who is standing before Him." But the Lord said to Samuel, "Do not look at the way he looks on the outside or how tall he is, because I have not chosen him. For the Lord does not look at the things man looks at. A man looks at the outside of a person, but the Lord looks at the heart."

1 SAMUEL 16:6–7

The human way we look at people and situations often makes us blind to seeing them from God's point of view. We see examples in today's passage. What other people thought about him was more powerful to Saul than his fear of God. And when Samuel looked at the outward appearance of David's brothers, God reminded him to look at their hearts. Ask God to help you see through His eyes. Doing so will surely change what you see.

THE LORD'S BATTLE
(1 Samuel 17)

MORNING PRAYER

Mighty God, if You count problems as enemies, I've battled with a few. But I've never fought anything as big and strong as Goliath. Was David so young and inexperienced that he didn't know the danger he faced? Or was he just so confident in You that he wasn't afraid? I want that kind of confidence—to face my enemies with faith, knowing You will help me win the battle. Lord, You are my strength. Amen.

EVENING DEVOTION

*Then David said to the Philistine, "You come to
me with a sword and spears. But I come to you in
the name of the Lord of All, the God of the armies
of Israel, Whom you have stood against."*
1 SAMUEL 17:45

David's courage came from his faith in God's power and his love for God's people. David knew without a doubt that God had a plan for His people and that He would deliver the Philistines into His hands that day. It's much easier to be brave when you know the battle will end in your favor. Through Jesus, you can be confident you will win in the end over death and sin. Every day, face the world armed with the power of Jesus, and you can't lose.

1 SAMUEL 18–19
JOHN 5:25–47
PSALM 80:1–7

SUNSHINE
(Psalm 80:1–7)

MORNING PRAYER

Oh God, Your love shines down on me like warm sunshine. You are like a shepherd guarding his sheep. You are my Shepherd and my protector. From Your throne in heaven You look down on me, seeing my every move. You light my path, and if I wander from it, You lead me back to You. God, I love You. Thank you for loving me. Amen.

EVENING DEVOTION

O God of all, bring us back to You. Make Your face shine upon us, and we will be saved.
PSALM 80:7

One of the coolest things to see is the sun breaking through the clouds after a storm. It's almost as if the very light of heaven is cutting through the dark clouds. You might think of the sunlight as God's face, His love shining down on you. Even on your darkest days God sees you and shines His love upon You like powerful rays of sunlight.

GOD KNOWS
(1 Samuel 20)

MORNING PRAYER

Dear Lord, reading about David and Jonathan's friendship is fascinating. It must have been hard for them to say goodbye. I've said goodbye to friends too. You've chosen different paths for us to follow. I pray that You will go with them and guide them in everything they do. Maybe, God, our paths will cross again someday. You are the only one who knows. Amen.

EVENING DEVOTION

Jesus looked up and saw many people coming to Him. He said to Philip, "Where can we buy bread to feed these people?" He said this to see what Philip would say. Jesus knew what He would do.
JOHN 6:5-6

In this passage in John, Jesus asked Philip a question. But He didn't ask it to learn the answer. In fact, John tells us that Jesus already knew what He was going to do. When God asks you to go through a difficult situation or poses questions that are hard to answer, take comfort in understanding that He already knows what He's going to do. Trust God to always do what is best. His way is perfect.

DAY 140

1 SAMUEL 22–23
JOHN 6:22–42
PSALM 81:1–10

BREAD OF LIFE
(John 6:30–40)

MORNING PRAYER

Jesus, You called Yourself "the Bread of Life." Your words are like healthy food. Everything You say is designed to give me strength and help me grow. Everything You do is for my good. As soon as I began to follow you, I felt stronger. I knew I was forgiven. I felt healthier because of Jesus! Fill me up with Your Spirit. You are the source of my energy and strength. Amen.

EVENING DEVOTION

Jesus said to them, "For sure, I tell you, you are not looking for Me because of the powerful works. You are looking for Me because you ate bread and were filled."
JOHN 6:26

It's easy to want more of God because of what He gives rather than for who He is. How often do you go to Him because you want something? God wants to give you good things, but even more, He wants you to want more of Him because he wants a strong relationship with you, like a father and son. He wants you to seek Him! When you do, He will fill you up with His power, strength, and love. God wants you to get to the place where you can't live without Him.

IMPRESSED WITH JESUS

(John 6:67–71)

MORNING PRAYER

Jesus, Peter knew You were the Messiah, God Himself. You had a human relationship with the disciples. They were Your friends. Still, they knew You were special. Peter said, "You have words that give life that lasts forever." The more time I spend with You, Jesus, the more I learn. The more I know of You, the more time I want to spend with You. You are my friend, my teacher, and my God. Amen.

EVENING DEVOTION

Simon Peter said to Him, "Lord, who else can we go to? You have words that give life that lasts forever."
JOHN 6:68

Peter soaked up all the teaching Jesus offered. Jesus was everything to Peter, and he couldn't imagine ever leaving Jesus for anything else. Have you been so impressed with Jesus that you can't imagine life without His friendship? Spend more time with Him. Get to know Jesus the way Peter did. A close relationship with Jesus is life-changing and, even better, everlasting. He will be the best friend you will ever have, and He will never leave you.

1 SAMUEL 25:32–27:12
JOHN 7:1–24
PSALM 82

PERFECT TIMING

(1 Samuel 26)

MORNING PRAYER

Dear God, I'm grateful no one hates me the way Saul did David. I can't imagine the sort of hate in which one person wants to kill another. If people dislike me, God, or hurt my feelings, help me to love them as You do. Keep me from wanting to hurt them back. You might have special plans to bring them into Your kingdom. Please use me to lead them to You. Amen.

EVENING DEVOTION

But David said to Abishai, "Do not destroy him. For who can put his hand out against the Lord's chosen one and not be guilty?" David said, "As the Lord lives, He will destroy him. Or his day will come to die. Or he will be killed in battle."
1 SAMUEL 26:9–10

David had learned to let God work out His perfect plan. David realized that God's plan stood alone and didn't have to match David's desires. Never assume that God wants what you want. That kind of thinking can lead you down the wrong path in a hurry! Pray. Seek God's will. Don't be in a rush to run on ahead of Him, doing what you want. His timing is perfect, and if you trust Him to show you His way, He will.

A SAVIOR
(John 8:1–11)

MORNING PRAYER

Jesus, I wonder what You wrote in the sand. You sent the woman's accusers away, reminding them that they were sinners too. You talked with the woman alone, forgiving her for her sin and reminding her not to sin again. I'm guilty of sinning too. When I judge others for what they do, remind me of the times I've done the wrong thing, Lord. Forgive me for my sins and help me not to sin again. Amen.

EVENING DEVOTION

Jesus stood up and said to her, "Woman, where are those who spoke against you? Has no man said you are guilty?"
JOHN 8:10

Can you imagine how afraid the woman in today's passage must have been to be dragged in front of Jesus—the expert on God's Law? The men wanted to kill her for what she had done. But Jesus, our Savior, judged her differently. You can be sure He would judge you the same way. Jesus wants to save you from sin. He is always ready to forgive when you mess up. Trust Him never to harm you and to always help you.

INVITATION
(Psalm 84:1–4)

MORNING PRAYER

God, when I invited You into my heart, You answered with a resounding, "Yes!" My heart became Your home; my body, Your temple. What I eat, how I dress, the things I do with my body—where I take it, whom I hang out with—all those things are important to You. I want a clean heart, a worthy place for You to live. With my body and soul, may I always honor You. Amen.

EVENING DEVOTION

My soul wants and even becomes weak from wanting to be in the house of the Lord. My heart and my flesh sing for joy to the living God.
PSALM 84:2

Do you desire God's presence as though it were the very thing holding you together? Being allowed into the presence of a ruler of any nation is an amazing honor. But God isn't any ruler. He is the King of kings, and He welcomes you into His presence whenever you want. Accept His invitation. God is always ready and waiting to spend time with you.

LIGHT VERSUS DARKNESS
(2 Samuel 2:1–4)

MORNING PRAYER

Lord, I wish I were patient like David. He didn't rush ahead, wanting to be king immediately. Instead, he asked You, "Is it time?" David had learned to wait, listen for Your words, and then obey. You want me to ask about every decision and need because You want to talk with me. You want me to learn to rely on Your timing and not my own. Thank You for reminding me, Lord. Amen.

EVENING DEVOTION

For the Lord God is a sun and a safe-covering. The Lord gives favor and honor. He holds back nothing good from those who walk in the way that is right.

PSALM 84:11

Whether we acknowledge it or not, we live in a battle of light versus darkness. God is our sun, never allowing the darkness to be so dark that it scares us. He is also our shield, protecting us from those who might want to hurt us. Think about that tonight as you fall asleep in the warm, soft light of His love.

2 SAMUEL 3–4
JOHN 9:13–34
PSALM 85:1–7

GOD'S WORK IN YOU
(Psalm 85:1–7)

MORNING PRAYER

Heavenly Father, today's scripture verse is about Your forgiveness. It says, "Give us life again" (Psalm 85:4). When we do things that displease You—when we sin—and come asking, "Give us life again," we rest on Jesus' promise that forgiveness is ours, no questions asked. Father, forgive my sins. Give me life again! Thank You for being kind to me and loving me. Amen.

EVENING DEVOTION

*The man who had been blind said to them, "I
do not know if He is a sinner or not. One thing
I know. I was blind, but now I can see."*
JOHN 9:25

The man in today's passage has a wonderful, simple testimony—the story of how he became a Christian. He once was blind but now he could see. And who made that happen? Jesus! Christ not only changed the man's body so he could see; He also changed the man's heart. The man became a Christian, a follower of Christ. Do you have a testimony? What led you to become a Christian?

DAY 147

DAVID DANCED
(2 Samuel 7:10–16)

MORNING PRAYER

Oh God, what a special friendship You had with David. He was a king, a great fighter for truth, a writer of poems and songs created to praise You. Obviously, he loved You deeply. Pour more of Your love into me. Give me a heart like David's—a heart filled to overflowing with Your love. God, I praise You. Amen.

EVENING DEVOTION

He was dancing before the Lord with all his strength. And he was wearing a linen vest.
2 SAMUEL 6:14

Dance like nobody's watching! That's what David did. He loved God so much and was so grateful for all God was doing that he did a dance of joy before God. David didn't worry about how he might look to anyone who saw him. He was so filled with happiness over God's goodness that he couldn't help but show it.

2 SAMUEL 7:18–10:19
JOHN 10:11–30
PSALM 86:1–10

DEEPLY LOVED
(John 10:11–30)

MORNING PRAYER

Lord Jesus, You are my Shepherd. I wonder if a sheep is a bit like a pet. A pet recognizes its owner's voice. A dog or cat comes when its owner calls its name. We are Your sheep. You want us to know Your voice and to listen to Your commands. Lord, when You say my name, I want to run to You, ready and happy that You want me by Your side. Amen.

EVENING DEVOTION

"I am the Good Shepherd. I know My sheep and My sheep know Me. I know My Father as My Father knows Me. I give My life for the sheep."
JOHN 10:14–15

The Good Shepherd knows you and loves you in ways you can't even imagine. He knew you perfectly before you were born. He knows each of your thoughts. Even when you displease Him, He still loves you. It's not a surface love either. Jesus loves you so much that He gave His life for you. You are completely known and deeply loved by the Person who matters most—Jesus.

BIGGER FAITH

(2 Samuel 12:1–25)

MORNING PRAYER

Dear God, David's story reminds me of times when my parents have corrected me. They pointed out something I had done wrong and explained why. I didn't always listen when they corrected me, and that got me into trouble. God, You are wise. Your Word explains to me right and wrong. When I mess up, correct me. Teach me to listen to You, obey You, and become more like You. Amen.

EVENING DEVOTION

"Because of you I am glad I was not there so that you may believe. Come, let us go to him."
JOHN 11:15

Sometimes God brings us through trouble to increase our faith. Jesus had healed so many people, yet He wasn't around to heal Lazarus. Jesus had an even bigger miracle planned. He planned not just to heal Lazarus but to raise him from the dead. When we feel like God hasn't done something in our lives, we need to remember that His plan is perfect. He may be getting ready for something bigger and better than we can imagine.

SORROW
(John 11:17–43)

MORNING PRAYER

Dearest Lord, Martha had extraordinary faith. Even after her brother died, when she was mourning his death, she received You and believed in Your goodness and power. When I am sad, Lord, sometimes I wonder where You are. I need to remember Martha and have faith that You are with me and will save me. Open my heart to You when I am sad. Comfort me with Your everlasting love. Amen.

EVENING DEVOTION

Jesus went to the grave with a sad heart. The grave was a hole in the side of a hill. A stone covered the door.
JOHN 11:38

Jesus was deeply grieved over Lazarus' death. He set an example for us, showing us that it is okay to feel sad. But in our sorrow, we need to remember that Jesus rose from the dead. Those who loved Him were overjoyed when they saw that He was alive. When sadness comes, we can count on Jesus to lead us to joy again, not only in this life but also on that day when we join Him in heaven.

FAR BETTER

(Psalm 88:1–9)

MORNING PRAYER

Jesus, I don't know how I got into this mess. It has made me feel tired, depressed, disappointed, and lonely. Sometimes I feel angry too. I'm hoping for a far better day today. I ask You to take away all the negative feelings and replace them with Your goodness. I ask for Your blessings today. Show me how I can make this mess better. My faith is in You. I trust You. Amen.

EVENING DEVOTION

The religious leaders of the Jews talked together about having Lazarus killed also. Because of Lazarus, many Jews were leaving their own religion. They were putting their trust in Jesus.
JOHN 12:10–11

There were men in the Jewish community who planned to kill not only Jesus but also Lazarus. All through history and on into the future, people have turned and will continue to turn against Jesus and do all they can to cause others to believe He doesn't exist. Those who believe in Jesus will be criticized. Still, it is far better to stand up for your belief in Jesus than it is to join those who don't believe.

DAY 152

2 SAMUEL 15:13–16:23
JOHN 12:20–43
PSALM 88:10–18

PERFECT LIFE
(2 Samuel 15:13–31)

MORNING PRAYER

Lord, give me the grace to approach You when I have a problem. Guide my steps. Help me find my way. Thank You for all the people in my life who love me and are ready to help me. I could really use someone to help me right now. I'm having trouble working through my problems by myself. I know You are with me, but will You send me a human helper too? Amen.

EVENING DEVOTION

"Anyone who loves his life will lose it. Anyone who hates his life in this world will keep it forever."
JOHN 12:25

If you put too much time and effort into making your life exactly how you want it here on earth, then you will certainly be disappointed. Reaching for the goal of a "perfect life" will lead you to live a life that's less than perfect. God is the only one who is perfect. You can have a good life here on earth by following Jesus and trying to be more like Him. Someday you will have a perfect life with Him in heaven.

KING
(John 13:1–5)

MORNING PRAYER

Dear Jesus, You loved Your disciples. You were King of all kings, yet You treated them like friends. You taught them about Your Father and showed them how to live their lives to please Him. You could have acted like a king, but instead You were humble and caring, even loving them enough to wash their feet. I know You love me too, Jesus. Every day, you treat me like a friend. Amen.

EVENING DEVOTION

*"I am your Teacher and Lord. I have washed your
feet. You should wash each other's feet also.
I have done this to show you what should be
done. You should do as I have done to you."*
JOHN 13:14–15

Jesus was a King who washed the feet of His followers and encouraged them to do the same for others. What kind of king would do this? Some people didn't believe that Jesus was the Messiah—the Savior—promised in the Old Testament. In His gentle, caring way, Jesus was more powerful than any earthly king. He cared deeply for His people, even to the point of giving His own life so they could be forgiven for their sins and have eternal life in heaven.

STILLER OF THE STORM
(2 Samuel 18:19–33)

MORNING PRAYER

Heavenly Father, hardly a day goes by when something doesn't get in my way. I don't like change. I get frustrated. I want everything to flow smoothly, and I want what's familiar. Forgive me. I trust in Your plan for me. Still the storm within me. Help me to stop fighting the changes You want for me. Give me the courage to follow wherever You lead. Amen.

EVENING DEVOTION

*You rule over the rising sea. When its
waves rise, You quiet them.*
PSALM 89:9

God is the only one who can control the wind and the waves of the sea. Today's psalm praises Him for doing so. In that moment when Jesus stilled the storm, on that day when He walked on water to be with His disciples, did they recognize that He was God? Did they remember the words of the psalmist: "You rule over the rising sea. When its waves rise, You quiet them"? We can only wonder.

ALWAYS PRESENT
(John 14:12–14)

MORNING PRAYER

Lord, when I pray, I sometimes end my prayer with "in Jesus' name." Your name has power! It is the name above all other names. Let me do whatever I do in the name of Jesus. I want to think, speak, and act to make others aware of You. And when I accomplish any good thing, I want to speak Your name—"All the credit goes to You, Jesus!" In Your name I pray. Amen.

EVENING DEVOTION

"Then I will ask My Father and He will give you another Helper. He will be with you forever."
JOHN 14:16

Throughout history, God had been moving closer to His people. But He couldn't possibly get any closer than when Jesus walked among them on earth, right? Jesus' disciples may have thought this, which is why Jesus told them about the comforter that the Father would send them. This comforter— the Holy Spirit—lives among us and also *in* us. He is Spirit, meaning He can be with all of us all at once, all the time. He is ever present with you now and forever.

YOUR LAMP
(2 Samuel 22:26–37)

MORNING PRAYER

Dear Lord, You are the lamp that lights my way. You've made a path just wide enough for me so I won't slip or get lost easily. Your way is perfect. With every step I take, I trust You more. The more I understand You, the more willing I am to follow Your path and see where it leads. Thank You, Lord, for lighting the way. Amen.

EVENING DEVOTION

*"For You are my lamp, O Lord. The Lord
gives light to my darkness."*
2 SAMUEL 22:29

David spoke from experience when he said God was his lamp in the darkness around him. His life wasn't easy. He had friends and family turn against him and force him into a life of running and hiding. But through even the darkest circumstances, God remained a faithful light by his side to shine on his steps and keep him safe from harm. No matter the situation, God is your lamp too. The darker it gets, the more brightly His light shines.

GOD IS TRUTH
(Psalm 89:30–37)

MORNING PRAYER

Dear God, everything around me is changeable. I'm change-able. But You're not. You are always the same. That's why I'm sure I can count on You. You will never leave me, even if I leave You. I can count on all Your promises as the truth. Most of all, I can count on Your love. I don't deserve all You give me. I'm so grateful to You, my ever-present, never-changing God. Amen.

EVENING DEVOTION

"I will always be faithful to him. I will not break My agreement, or change what was spoken by My lips."
PSALM 89:33–34

God made an agreement with His servant David, and He stands by that agreement for all time. When God makes an agreement, it's a promise. God's promise is always perfect, and He never goes back on any promise He makes. You can believe that as the absolute truth.

1 KINGS 1
JOHN 16:23–17:5
PSALM 89:38–52

TAKE HOPE!
(John 16:33)

MORNING PRAYER

Jesus, You say when I have trouble in this world I can find peace in You. I'm filled with comfort and hope, knowing that when I face trouble, I can run to You. I can overcome any problem with You by my side. If I just have faith and anchor myself to Your love, I know I will find peace. I can rest even when life doesn't go my way. Amen.

EVENING DEVOTION

*"I have told you these things so you may have peace
in Me. In the world you will have much trouble.
But take hope! I have power over the world!"*
JOHN 16:33

Jesus told His disciples two truths: first, that in the world they would have trouble, and second, even in trouble they would find peace because Jesus had overcome the world. Don't be surprised when trouble comes into your life. Jesus warned us trouble would come. But take hope! In Jesus, you will find a kind of peace unlike anything this world can offer.

HE PRAYED FOR YOU
(John 17:20–26)

MORNING PRAYER

Lord, at the Last Supper, You prayed for me and for everyone who believes in You. You prayed that we would love one another and that we would see Your greatness. You prayed that we would be one with You. I want to live Your prayer, Jesus. I will do my best to love others, and in the ways I talk and act, I hope they will see You in me. Amen.

EVENING DEVOTION

*"I do not pray for these followers only. I
pray for those who will put their trust in Me
through the teaching they have heard."*
JOHN 17:20

When you read today's scripture, did you realize the prayer Jesus prayed was for you? Just hours before His death, Jesus prayed for you. At the Last Supper, He made it clear in His prayer that He wasn't just praying for the men at the table. He prayed for all His followers for all the years to come. And one of those followers is *you*.

DAY 160

1 KINGS 3–4
JOHN 18:1–27
PSALM 90:13–17

A BETTER PLAN
(1 Kings 3:6–14)

MORNING PRAYER

Lord, Solomon asked to know the difference between right and wrong. I need that kind of wisdom too. Sometimes I think I can tell others what to do—but then I realize that I have trouble taking care of my own problems. Lord, give me the kind of wisdom that only comes from You. Amen.

EVENING DEVOTION

"So give Your servant an understanding heart to judge Your people and know the difference between good and bad. For who is able to judge Your many people?"
1 KINGS 3:9

Wouldn't our prayers be better if we stopped praying for things to turn out the way we wanted them to and instead prayed for wisdom and understanding? Wisdom comes with knowing that God's plan, whatever it is, is so much better than our plan. So when you pray, ask God for wisdom and patience to understand His will.

STAND STRONG

(John 18:28–40)

MORNING PRAYER

Dearest Jesus, even when You stood before Pilate, You stood strong, proclaiming who You were. You said You came to speak about the truth and that everyone who is of the truth hears Your voice. The truth is. . .You are God! Pilate might not have understood that, but I do. You are my God, and I will stand strong and proclaim You. I will never be shy in telling others about You. Amen.

EVENING DEVOTION

*A thousand may fall at your side, and ten thousand
at your right hand. But it will not come near you.*
PSALM 91:7

Psalm 91 is a powerful psalm about God's loving protection. It teaches that nothing on earth has power over you because you are a son of God. If you remember that, then you will realize you have a wall of protection around you. God is always with you. In any kind of trouble, you can count on Him. When trouble comes your way, stand strong. Your heavenly Father is with you, and He is all the protection you need.

JESUS IS KING

(Psalm 91:11–16)

MORNING PRAYER

Jesus, when You went to the cross, You were willing to suffer even though you are the King of kings. That's who You are—both God and man. When I call on You, You will answer me. You will bring me out of my troubles and keep me safe. You will even honor me. I pray that my love and trust for You will grow. The more of You I know and love, the more blessed I am. Amen.

EVENING DEVOTION

This was read by many of the Jews. The place where Jesus was nailed to the cross was near the city. The writing was written in the Hebrew and the Latin and the Greek languages. Then the head religious leaders of the Jews said to Pilate, "Do not write, 'The King of the Jews'! Write, 'He said, I am the King of the Jews.'" Pilate said, "What I have written is to stay just as it is!"
JOHN 19:20–22

Even during Christ's humiliating death, it was proclaimed to all who passed by that Jesus was King. The truth about Him can never be silenced, not even by the angry mob who killed the Son of God. If you face persecution, mockery, or hostility at school or even from friends for your faith, know that you are in good company with your Savior.

MEETING GOD
(1 Kings 8:1–53)

MORNING PRAYER

Dear God, nothing can hold You back. You live inside my heart, and from there, You spill out of me to others. The more I try to be like Jesus, the more others will see You in me. If I use my words to tell others about You, they will meet You and hopefully receive You into their hearts too. Lord, You have no boundaries. Your love grows wherever You go. Amen.

EVENING DEVOTION

When the religious leaders came from the holy place, the cloud filled the house of the Lord.
1 KINGS 8:10

How awesome it must have been to see God's Spirit in the cloud fill the holy place. Imagine being one of the people standing there seeing God, knowing He was right there with you. Thanks to Jesus, you can go directly to the throne of God each time you pray. You can always meet with your heavenly Father. His spirit lives in You, so He is present with you all the time.

LIFE WELL LIVED
(1 Kings 9:1–9)

MORNING PRAYER

Lord God, my purpose is to bring honor to Your name. You are watching over me. You care about me and You're proud of me. I will do my best to honor You in all I do. I want to be a man like Jesus, doing what is right and acting in goodness and truth. I'm nowhere as perfect as Jesus, Father, so forgive me when I fail. Pick me up and let me try again. Amen.

EVENING DEVOTION

They will still give fruit when they are old.
They will be full of life and strength.
PSALM 92:14

Older people, those who are your grandparents' age, often have much wisdom to share from their long and faithful walk with Jesus. Seek out the older people in your life. Ask them to tell you what they have learned by following Jesus. Listen closely to their answers. Wisdom is hidden in their words. When you find it, hold on to it. As you grow in age and in wisdom, the words of these older people will remain in your heart.

ABUNDANT LIFE
(Psalm 93)

MORNING PRAYER

Oh God, You are the greatest of all kings. You sat on Your throne before time began. You created everything and You are more powerful than anything on earth. What You say will happen can't be undone. Your laws can't be changed. You will reign forever. I am so grateful to be Your son! You have promised me everything in Your kingdom. Heaven is waiting for me—and so are You. Amen.

EVENING DEVOTION

But these are written so you may believe that Jesus is the Christ, the Son of God. When you put your trust in Him, you will have life that lasts forever through His name.
JOHN 20:31

There is not enough room in the Gospels—the Bible books of Matthew, Mark, Luke, and John—to tell about all the people whose lives were changed by Jesus. But we've been given enough to believe, all these years later, in the Man who touched and changed real people's lives. Write down the ways Jesus has changed and is changing you. Remembering His faithfulness will make you stronger in the future and lead to a fuller and more joyful life.

A POWERFUL SAY

(John 21)

MORNING PRAYER

Lord Jesus, when You ask me, *"Do you love Me?"* I say I do. But do I love You more than the things surrounding me—my friends and family, my pets, my phone and video games? Open my eyes to the things I'm grasping too tightly, all the things I've made more important than You. Please forgive me and help me to love You even more. Amen.

EVENING DEVOTION

But Rehoboam turned away from the wise words the leaders gave him. Instead he spoke with the young men who grew up with him and stood by him.
1 KINGS 12:8

Rehoboam very unwisely followed the counsel of his foolish friends rather than the advice of the older men who had far more experience as rulers. Who are your counselors? Whose thoughts and attitudes are rubbing off on you? Choose wisely your friends and those you go to for advice. Remember that those who are closest to you have a powerful influence on your life.

CORRECTION

(Acts 1:8)

MORNING PRAYER

Dear God, everyone knows people who don't believe in You. I pray for them, starting with the people I see every day—my family members, classmates, friends, and neighbors. I pray for people all over the world who don't believe in You. Please open their eyes. Use me as Your helper. I want to tell others about You, and I pray they will see You through me. Amen.

EVENING DEVOTION

Happy is the man who is punished until he gives up sin, O Lord, and whom You teach from Your Law.
PSALM 94:12

Have you thought of discipline as a blessing? Sometimes when you have a nagging feeling in your heart that you've done something to displease God, it might be His way of trying to get your attention. God teaches you right from wrong through the Bible. He wants you to obey. If you don't, He will correct you. And when He corrects you, He is pulling you back from taking the wrong path—that's the blessing!

GOD DOESN'T
CHANGE HIS MIND

(Acts 1:12–26)

MORNING PRAYER

Lord Jesus, Matthias seems like a decent, average guy. He wasn't up front like Paul—maybe he really preferred to work behind the scenes. There are many different ways of serving You, and I don't have to be anything other than what You call me to be. I will work my heart out for You, Jesus! I just want to serve You. Amen.

EVENING DEVOTION

But the Lord his God gave him a lamp in Jerusalem because of David. He gave him a son to rule after him and to keep Jerusalem strong.

1 KINGS 15:4

God doesn't abandon His plans. He promised David that one of his descendants would always reign. Even with all the evil kings who reigned after David, God did not go back on His promise. Jesus, a descendant of David, came to reign forever. You serve a God who keeps His promises and doesn't change His mind. You can be certain that no matter what is happening in your life right now, it is definitely part of God's perfect plan.

SING TO THE LORD
(Psalm 96:1)

MORNING PRAYER

Dear God, I sing praises to You this morning. I will praise You every morning of my life because You are so good to me. You've put a song in my heart—the joy of knowing Jesus! I want to share that song with everyone I know. God, I want to add to the choir of believers. Show me that one person today who needs to hear the good news. Amen.

EVENING DEVOTION

Sing to the Lord a new song. Let all the earth sing to the Lord.
PSALM 96:1

The person who wrote this psalm wanted all the earth to sing to the Lord. Many years later, at Pentecost, this became a reality. The Holy Spirit arrived, allowing people from many nations to hear the gospel. The good news about Jesus continued to spread all around the world. One day, believers from every nation will be singing God's praises together in heaven. What a powerful sound it will be!

DAY 170

THE TRUE GOD
(1 Kings 19:9–17)

MORNING PRAYER

Lord God, I am thankful that just as You met with Elijah on the mountain, You will meet with me today to protect me, save me, and provide for my needs. I should always listen when You speak. When You ask me the same question twice, I had better pay double attention. Your gentle whisper is as powerful as a cyclone. Speak to me, God. What can I do for You today? Amen.

EVENING DEVOTION

"Answer me, O Lord. Answer me so these people may know that You, O Lord, are God. Turn their hearts to You again." Then the fire of the Lord fell. It burned up the burnt gift, the wood, the stones and the dust. And it picked up the water that was in the ditch.
1 KINGS 18:37–38

Elijah stood up and spoke against the enemies of God. But when it came time for him to show Israel who the true God was, his prayer was a powerful picture of someone who walked humbly with God and had a personal relationship with Him. God's fire burned up the sacrifice, not so Elijah would look good, but so people would know God's power. He shattered the crowd's disbelief by sending down fire from heaven.

POWER OF THE CREATOR
(Psalm 97:1–6)

MORNING PRAYER

Almighty God, You are the great Creator of earth. The Bible says, "Let the earth be full of joy. Let the sea and all that is in it make a loud noise. Let the fields and all that is in them be full of joy. Then all the trees of the land will sing for joy" (Psalm 96:11–12). Your power is known throughout the universe. I praise You, Lord. The whole earth praises You. Amen.

EVENING DEVOTION

He jumped up on his feet and walked. Then he went into the house of God with them. He gave thanks to God as he walked.
ACTS 3:8

The change in this lame man is an example of God's ability to completely transform a person. Not only did God fix what was wrong in the man's legs, but He also created muscle strength and coordination that the man never had. Even with all the incredible medical and scientific advancements we have been blessed with, we can never match the power of the Creator to restore His broken creation. God is so worthy of praise!

A HEART LIKE HIS

(1 Kings 21)

MORNING PRAYER

Dear God, what a surprise to discover that the evil King Ahab repented. He did more to lead Your people further from You than any other king in Israel's history. But when he said he was sorry, You listened. You forgave him. I take comfort in Your amazing grace. If You could forgive an evil king, then I know I can trust You to forgive me as well. Amen.

EVENING DEVOTION

*Let those who love the Lord hate what is bad. For
He keeps safe the souls of His faithful ones. He
takes them away from the hand of the sinful.*
PSALM 97:10

Do you sometimes see the world as messed up? Evil exists here, but still, the earth is your home until you join God in heaven. It's good that you see the messiness. It's a sign that you love God and know right from wrong. God hates the messes even more than you do. But as your heart becomes more like His, you will learn to see the world more from His perspective. Ask Him to continue to mold your heart to be more like His.

PURE AND HOLY
(Acts 4:23–31)

MORNING PRAYER

Father, I pray to have a bold faith like that of the early believers. Even when the world stood against them, people like Peter and John weren't afraid to share with others that You are the Messiah, our Savior, sent to forgive our sins and make a path for us to heaven. God, I pray for courage when I tell others about You. Give me a heart that is strong and bold. Amen.

EVENING DEVOTION

For He is coming to say who is guilty or not on the earth. He will be right in what He decides about the world. And He will be fair to the people.

PSALM 98:9

On earth, people are often judged unfairly. Humans point at each other and accuse each other of many things. But God isn't that kind of judge. He is always fair. He doesn't take into account skin color, age, nationality, or gender. His judgment is pure and holy. Someday Jesus will come to earth again and wipe out evil. He will lead everyone on earth to live together in peace.

LIFE GIVING
(2 Kings 2:11–12)

MORNING PRAYER

Dear Lord, when I pray for something big and it doesn't happen, it can feel like part of me died. But I've learned that when You say no to a prayer it's because You have something better waiting for me—a new and life-giving part of Your plan. Do You have something new for me to do? Whatever it is, prepare me. I am willing, Lord. Show me the way. Amen.

EVENING DEVOTION

"We told you not to teach about Christ! See! You are spreading this teaching over all Jerusalem. Now you are making it look as if we are guilty of killing this Man."
ACTS 5:28

The apostles' constant preaching of the gospel was so effective that city leaders took note and felt something had to be done to address the rapid spread of their teachings. Wouldn't it be amazing if we could fill the cities we live in with this same kind of life-giving preaching? To be accused of preaching the gospel as effectively as these faithful and courageous apostles would truly be an honor.

IN NEED
(Acts 6:1–7)

MORNING PRAYER

God, forgive me when I try to do life on my own. Open my eyes to the times I need help. Lead me to find guidance from those who are wiser than me. When someone offers to help me, let me also offer to help someone else. I want to be an active member of "Team God," sharing with others my time, talents, love, prayers, encouragement, and belief in You. Amen.

EVENING DEVOTION

Then he said, "Go around and get jars from all your neighbors. Get empty jars, many of them. Then go in and shut the door behind you and your sons. Pour the oil into all these jars, and set aside each one that is full."
2 KINGS 4:3–4

Could Elisha, through God's power, have solved all the widow's problems in today's passage without having her do anything? Of course he could have. But instead, the Bible gives us a valuable model of helping those in need. The woman first worked to get empty jars from all her neighbors, and then God performed the miracle. God knew that sometimes it's good to allow the person in need to be part of the solution and not just a bystander who gets the reward.

2 KINGS 5:1–6:23
ACTS 7:1–16
PSALM 101

NEVER ALONE
(Psalm 101)

MORNING PRAYER

Lord God, Joshua said, "As for me and my family, we will serve the Lord" (Joshua 24:15). That's what I want, for my whole family to serve You. Shower Your love on my family members. Surround them with people who know and love You, people who will lead them to You. Through faith in Jesus, add those who don't believe to Your kingdom. Don't leave any of them alone. Make my whole family one with You. Amen.

EVENING DEVOTION

He answered, "Do not be afraid. For those who are
with us are more than those who are with them." Then
Elisha prayed and said, "O Lord, I pray, open his eyes,
that he may see." And the Lord opened the servant's
eyes, and he saw. He saw that the mountain was full
of horses and war-wagons of fire all around Elisha.
2 KINGS 6:16–17

Oh, that God would open our eyes as He did the eyes of Elisha's servant, that we too might see the army of protection surrounding us as we do God's will. We are never alone in carrying out the will of God. His heavenly army is all around us leading us and giving us courage. Remember that truth whenever something blocks your way. You are not alone. You have a whole army ready to help you smash through that barrier.

GOD CAN USE YOU
(2 Kings 6:24–7:2)

MORNING PRAYER

Lord, I don't like waiting through bad times. I want You to solve my problems right away. Forgive me when I get upset with You. I trust in Your promises. I know You will bring me through my trouble to better days. Make my faith stronger. Help me to trust in Your perfect timing. And in the meantime, please help me to stay calm. Provide me with peace. Thank You, Lord. Amen.

EVENING DEVOTION

"He saw one of the Jews being hurt. Moses helped the Jew and killed the man from Egypt."
ACTS 7:24

God doesn't just save those who are already perfect and have their act together. In fact, the three men who wrote the most books of the Bible were all murderers—Moses (as we read about in today's passage), David (who killed Uriah), and Paul (who looked on in approval as Stephen was murdered). These three men of faith were far from perfect men, and yet God used them to carry out His perfect plan. If He could use them, He can certainly use you.

GOD IS FOREVER
(Psalm 102:8–17)

MORNING PRAYER

Heavenly Father, I'm so grateful that Jesus will reign on His throne forever. He is King of kings and Lord of lords both on earth and in heaven. Jesus is here now. He always has been here. He will be here every day for as long as the earth exists. Thank You, God, for the gift of Your Son, Jesus, and for His gift of eternal life. Amen.

EVENING DEVOTION

My days are like the evening shadow. I dried up like grass. But You and Your name, O Lord, will always be forever and to all people for all time.
PSALM 102:11–12

The author of today's passage understood how weak humans are. He knew his life was fragile like a flickering shadow or grass that withers in the sun. But he had faith in Someone greater than himself. One day the author won't be remembered on earth, but God will be remembered and praised for as long as the earth lasts—and then for eternity. While you exist here on earth, put all your effort into doing God's work. Help others to see His greatness.

ALL AROUND THE WORLD

(Acts 7:54–60)

MORNING PRAYER

Jesus, in times when I feel alone, I want to remember Stephen seeing You standing by Your Father's right hand. Romans 8:28 says, "We know that God makes all things work together for the good of those who love Him and are chosen to be a part of His plan." When times are hard, I know You will somehow work everything out to bring about good. Thank You, Jesus, for always standing by and with me. Amen.

EVENING DEVOTION

*Those who had been made to go to other
places preached the Word as they went.*
ACTS 8:4

Those who preached the gospel in the days of the early Church faced ill-treatment and punishment for their faith. But that didn't stop God's plan. In fact, God used the mistreatment of His people to reach others for Christ more quickly. Had those Christians preaching the gospel not been forced from their homes, it would have taken longer for the good news to spread around the world.

A PLACE IN GOD'S FAMILY
(2 Kings 13:4–5)

MORNING PRAYER

Father, I've picked up some bad habits. I wish I could get rid of them once and for all. But too often I mess up a second, third, and fourth time. Again and again I call on You, asking for forgiveness. Please show me how to get in step with Your will so I can get rid of these habits forever. Help me to win the battle. Fight for me, God. Amen.

EVENING DEVOTION

Philip said, "If you believe with all your heart, you may." The man said, "I believe that Jesus Christ is the Son of God."
ACTS 8:37

Maybe sometimes you feel like you don't belong, or maybe you know someone else who feels this way. Maybe you have seen a homeless person and wondered if he or she has a family. No one is truly alone in this world—God loves and wants them. The sad thing is that not everyone knows this. That's why it's important to let others know that God is their Father and that He is ready to welcome them into His family forever, where they will be dearly loved.

NOT YOUR OWN EFFORT

(Acts 9:1–16)

MORNING PRAYER

Lord Jesus, You told Ananias to take Saul into his home. Ananias knew this was a dangerous command. Saul hated Christians and wanted to kill them. Yet Ananias obeyed. When You direct me to go a certain way, I want to be like Ananias and obey You. I know all Your plans are perfect. I trust You to guide me, Lord, even when I'm afraid of what lies ahead. Amen.

EVENING DEVOTION

*For He knows what we are made of. He
remembers that we are dust.*
PSALM 103:14

God knows you aren't perfect. He knows that sometimes you will mess up. He knows that sometimes you will be afraid to follow where He leads you. What God wants is for you to do your best to obey and serve Him. Through no effort of your own, He can lead you to do something great. So don't allow thoughts about your imperfection to get in the way of your service to Him.

DAY 182

ACTS 9:17–31
PSALM 103:15–22

SAVED BY GRACE
(Psalm 103:15–22)

MORNING PRAYER

Dear Savior, this morning all I want to do is praise You. With my whole heart, soul, and strength, I praise You! You came into this world to teach me the way to You. You gave Your life so I can live forever in heaven in complete and total perfection. Oh Lord, how wonderful You are! How grateful I am to You for everything. I will praise You today and every day of my life. Amen.

EVENING DEVOTION

Then Barnabas took him to the missionaries. He told them that Saul had seen the Lord on the road. He told them also how the Lord had spoken to Saul and how he had preached without fear in Damascus in the name of Jesus.
Acts 9:27

God will build His church. Sometimes He builds it by changing the hearts of His enemies, people like Saul. But more often He builds it through the faithful service of His children, people like Barnabas and Ananias. The day you accepted Jesus into your heart, you received a miracle. God welcomed you into His church—you joined all the world's believers—and He began using you to share the gospel and help Him to work His plan.

MIRACLE WORKER

(Acts 10)

MORNING PRAYER

God, use me to increase Your kingdom here on earth. You want everyone to believe in You. It doesn't matter who they are or where they live. You want everyone alive today to know You and receive Your gift of eternal life in heaven. What can I do today to lead others to You? Is there a friend who needs to hear about You? I'm listening, God. Tell me what to do. Amen.

EVENING DEVOTION

Peter went back with them. When he came, they took him to the room. All the women whose husbands had died were standing around crying. They were showing the clothes Dorcas had made while she was with them.
ACTS 9:39

Peter was called to Joppa because another faithful servant of God had died. This servant, Dorcas, hadn't given sight to the blind or raised anyone from the dead, but her work was so important that a group of people begged Peter to bring her back to life. God allowed Peter to answer their prayer. God sometimes works through miracles, but He often works through people like Dorcas, a faithful child of God who made clothing for those in need.

DAY 184

2 KINGS 19:8–20:21
ACTS 10:17–33
PSALM 104:10–23

MIGHTIER THAN FEAR ITSELF
(2 Kings 19:14–19)

MORNING PRAYER

Heavenly Father, make me aware of any lies people have told about You. Keep me from ever doubting that You exist or that You are not who You say You are. I believe You are the almighty God. Everything You say is the truth. You keep Your promises, and You don't make mistakes. If anything ever pulls me away from You, lead me back. Protect me, God, from lies. Hold me firm in Your truth. Amen.

EVENING DEVOTION

Hezekiah took the letter from the hand of the men from Assyria, and read it. Then he went up to the house of the Lord, and spread the letter out before the Lord.
2 KINGS 19:14

Fear is a powerful weapon. The Assyrians understood this as they attempted to destroy the peace of God's people with terrifying lies. But fear is no match for God. Hezekiah did what we all should do when faced with a powerful enemy. He laid the whole situation before God. He didn't try to figure it out on his own. Instead, he went to Someone mightier than himself and mightier than fear itself.

GOD'S CHILDREN
(2 Kings 22)

MORNING PRAYER

Dear God, forgive me the times I think I know how things are supposed to get done. When Josiah's helpers cleaned the temple, they thought they had been doing things right until they read Your Word again. Sometimes I mess up and forget what the Bible tells me. Teach me. Lead me through the Bible so I will learn. And I will do my best to obey You. Amen.

EVENING DEVOTION

Peter said, "I can see, for sure, that God does not respect one person more than another. He is pleased with any man in any nation who honors Him and does what is right."
Acts 10:34–35

The Roman soldier Cornelius sent men to visit Peter. What seems like a simple story in the book of Acts was really something new and beautiful for God's kingdom. From this point forward, Gentiles—non-Jewish people—were openly welcomed to accept Jesus' gift of salvation. People from all nations were allowed the blessing of becoming children of God.

HEART, SOUL, AND MIGHT
(Psalm 104:31–35)

MORNING PRAYER

Father God, I can imagine us taking a walk together outside. I listen as You share stories and words of wisdom with me. I love hearing You say that You are proud of me and that You welcome the times we spend together. I give You my full attention. God, I am never happier or more at peace than when I am with You. Amen.

EVENING DEVOTION

Before Josiah there was no king like him who turned to the Lord with all his heart and soul and strength, obeying all the Law of Moses. And no one like him came after him.
2 KINGS 23:25

Josiah understood who he was and who God was. The title and position of king did not make Josiah think he was equal to his heavenly King. He knew that all understanding and guidance come from the Lord. He turned to God with all his heart, soul, and strength. Have you done the same?

DECLARE IT!
(Psalm 105:1-7)

MORNING PRAYER

Lord God, sometimes I have no words to describe You. Who You are is beyond words. *Grand? Glorious?* Not good enough. When I think about all You've created, all the ways You do what is right and true, and all the times You've shown Your love to me, there are no words. The best I can do is praise You forever. With whatever words I have, I will spend my whole life telling others about You. Amen.

EVENING DEVOTION

O give thanks to the Lord. Call on His name. Make His works known among the people. Sing to Him. Sing praises to Him. Tell of all His great works.
PSALM 105:1-2

Though your relationship with God is deeply personal, it should not be totally private. You should openly give thanks to God and tell others what He has done for you. If you truly understood the depth of His grace to you, you wouldn't be able to keep to yourself your praise or love for Him. So talk about Him, and tell everyone you know about the wonderful things He does.

DAY 188

1 CHRONICLES 1–2
ACTS 13:14–43
PSALM 105:8–15

AS NUMEROUS AS THE STARS
(Acts 13:14–43)

MORNING PRAYER

Jesus, when the apostle Paul spoke about You, people wanted to know more. I want to speak of You the way Paul did, bravely. I want to reach people who haven't heard about You. When I talk or text with my friends, Jesus, give me the words to tell them about You. Open their ears to hear and their hearts to welcome You. Amen.

EVENING DEVOTION

He has remembered His agreement forever, the promise He made to last through a thousand families-to-come.
PSALM 105:8

God promised Abraham that his descendants would be as numerous as the stars. Abraham probably couldn't have imagined how perfectly God would fulfill that promise. God has remembered His promise and gathered countless spiritual descendants of Abraham from all over the earth. Because of your faith in God, you are a direct fulfillment of God's promise.

CIRCUMSTANCES

(1 Chronicles 4:9–10)

MORNING PRAYER

Lord, forgive me for the times when I let circumstances hold me back from following You with all my heart. When I'm tired and ready to give up, You give me strength to keep going. I want to be like Jabez. He didn't wait for relief from pain before he went to work. Instead, he got busy. You have things for me to do, Lord. I won't let circumstances get in my way. Amen.

EVENING DEVOTION

The missionaries were filled with joy and with the Holy Spirit.
Acts 13:52

First Chronicles 4:10 tells us about Jabez, whose prayer for blessing, success, and protection was granted. We can imagine he would have lived a happy and joyful life. In Acts, we read about Jesus' followers who were mistreated and imprisoned, and yet even then they were filled with joy. Why? Because God had considered them worthy to suffer for the sake of Jesus. When it comes to living a joy-filled life, circumstances don't matter. Whom you serve does.

GOD-GIVEN TALENTS

(1 Chronicles 5:18)

MORNING PRAYER

Dear God, You create in each of us special skills and talents—things we do well. We didn't choose them; You gave them to us. Our choice is whether or not to use them. I want to use what I'm good at to serve You. Make me aware of any hidden skills I need to polish. Bring teachers and others into my life who can help me improve on my talents even more. Amen.

EVENING DEVOTION

"Why are you doing this? We are only men with feelings like yours. We preach the Good News that you should turn from these empty things to the living God. He made the heavens and the earth and the sea and everything in them."

ACTS 14:15

Paul and Barnabas might not have been mistreated if they allowed the people to keep on thinking they were gods. But they didn't take the easy way out by turning from the real God. Instead, they said they were only men—human. God could (and sometimes does) send angels to tell others who He is, but most often He uses imperfect, weak humans. Through these "broken vessels"—imagine broken jars—He can shine the light of His power more clearly.

PROMISED LAND
(Acts 15:1–18)

MORNING PRAYER

Heavenly Father, my friends and I sometimes disagree about what a Bible verse means. I guess that's because we rely on our own ideas, thoughts, and experiences. Help me to see the Bible through the eyes of others. We might learn from each other by looking at each other's ideas, and the world, differently. Above all, God, open our eyes to Your truth. Amen.

EVENING DEVOTION

He gave them the lands of the nations. They were given what others had worked for, so that they might do what He told them and keep His Law. Praise the Lord!
PSALM 105:44–45

It was a miracle God brought the Israelites through the wilderness and into the rich land He'd promised them. The journey was rough. The people made it more difficult for themselves when they disobeyed and disappointed God. Don't make the same mistakes they did. When life gets hard, keep turning to God and following Him. He knows the way to your promised land. His whole kingdom awaits you someday. Thank Him. Serve Him. Follow Him.

SEPARATE WAYS

(Psalm 106:1–3)

MORNING PRAYER

God, You are so good. You have done more for me than I can put into words. So often I'm amazed by the ways You work in my life and the good things You do for me. When I obey You and do what is right, You reward me. Father, keep moving me forward with Your love. Give me even more reasons to praise You every day. Amen.

EVENING DEVOTION

They argued so much that they left each other. Barnabas took John Mark with him and went by ship to the island of Cyprus.
ACTS 15:39

Two apostles who were working together to spread the gospel had such a strong disagreement that they decided to separate. But God used even this for His purposes. Instead of working side by side, Paul and Barnabas were more effective by going their separate ways and spreading the gospel to different places and people. If you and a friend disagree, do your best to fix it. But if you end up going your separate ways, know that God has a plan for you both.

GLORIOUS GOD

(Acts 16:6–10)

MORNING PRAYER

Lord, sometimes I try to reach a goal but everything I do fails. Usually, I end up disappointed or even giving up. Today's Bible passage helps me realize that when my own ways fail, I need to remember to turn to You. When I've tried everything I know to do, You might have a path I haven't explored, a different way for me to go, or even a different goal. Lead me, Lord! I'm ready to follow. Amen.

EVENING DEVOTION

*They traded their shining-greatness for something
that looked like a bull that eats grass.*
PSALM 106:20

It seems absurd the Israelites created an idol of a common animal to replace the God whose very presence they had witnessed in the pillar of fire and cloud. But don't we often do the same thing? We trade everything we know about God and His power and create our own idols—things we honor and respect more than Him. We reduce God to a sort of genie we run to when we want something. Don't ever forget who you serve: the all-powerful God of the universe.

FAR GREATER
(Psalm 106:30–31)

MORNING PRAYER

Dear God, I don't know where You will lead me. As I mature, You might nudge me out of my comfort zone and ask me to act boldly in Your honor. I pray that I'll be up to it. I want to serve You well, God, without being afraid. Will You provide me with godly friends to help me? Together, we can encourage one another whenever we hesitate or feel afraid. Amen.

EVENING DEVOTION

The girl's owners saw that they could not make money with her anymore. Then they took hold of Paul and Silas and dragged them to the leaders. This happened in the center of town where people gather.
ACTS 16:19

The idea of Jesus might not bother most people—until He gets in the way of their comfort. We live in a world where comfort and success are gods. The Jesus we know may make people uncomfortable because He makes them aware of their sin and asks them to give up things they love. The riches found in Jesus are far greater than any here on earth. We can't risk not sharing Jesus with others because we're afraid of how they might react.

UPSIDE DOWN
(1 Chronicles 16)

MORNING PRAYER

Dear God, I think about all the people around the world who sing their praises to You. From Bible times until now, music and songs have been used to honor You, telling the history of Your goodness and love. Father, this morning I sing to You my songs of praise. Oh, how great You are! Amen.

EVENING DEVOTION

But they did not find them there. Then they dragged Jason and some other Christians out in front of the leaders and cried out, "These men who have been making trouble over all the world have come here also."
ACTS 17:6

The apostles were accused of turning the world upside down. How incredible would it be if those words were spoken today about God's people? What if people were less afraid to stand up for God and His truths, even when faced with opposition? Jesus is the only way to turn lives around, to turn bad to good—to turn the world upside down.

CULTURE
(Psalm 106:44–48)

MORNING PRAYER

Dear God, I love how You work through other people. You've used my parents to discipline me and teach me about forgiveness. You've used friends to bring joy into my life and to support and comfort me. I want to be a blessing to others the way they've been a blessing to me. Use me to build them up. Allow me to be the channel You use to reach and teach them. Amen.

EVENING DEVOTION

"It is in Him that we live and move and keep on living. Some of your own men have written, 'We are God's children.'"
ACTS 17:28

Paul knew and understood the culture in which he was preaching. In today's passage, he even quoted the society's poets. It's important to know the people you're talking to when sharing the gospel so you can shape your message in a way that is easily understandable to their culture. Be careful, though, not to change the meaning of God's Word.

TRAINING
(1 Chronicles 21)

MORNING PRAYER

Heavenly Father, if You loved David, who made plenty of mistakes in his life, then I know You love me. As he grew older, David became wiser. He took responsibility for the times he messed up. You continued to form him into the person You wanted him to be. I know You will do the same for me. Work on me, God. Make me stronger and wiser each day. Amen.

EVENING DEVOTION

*Satan stood up against Israel, and
moved David to number Israel.*
1 CHRONICLES 21:1

Today's passage in 1 Chronicles is one of the few times Satan is mentioned in the Old Testament. But even when his name isn't there, you'll see his evil work in many Bible stories. It's important to remember that a spiritual battle—a war between bad and good—is taking place in the world today. We need to be ready to fight on God's side. Satan, the enemy, is real. So be on your guard. And remember that God is far more powerful than anything Satan can do.

BE A FIXER
(Acts 18:24–28)

MORNING PRAYER

Heavenly Father, some people make the words in the Bible fit what they want instead of holding to the truth of what Your words mean. Please teach me to know the difference between false teaching and the truth. Give me patience to listen to new ideas and courage to speak up for what I know is true. Bring people into my life who know and will teach me the true meaning of Your words. Amen.

EVENING DEVOTION

He began to speak without fear in the Jewish place of worship. Aquila and Priscilla heard him. They took him to their house and taught him much more about the things of God.
ACTS 18:26

When Aquila and Priscilla heard Apollos speak, they knew he didn't really understand the gospel. Instead of walking away and laughing at him, Aquila and Priscilla stayed and taught Apollos the truth about Jesus' gift of forever life in heaven. Wouldn't it be great if we spent less time talking about a problem and more time working to fix it?

INSPIRED
(Psalm 107:20)

MORNING PRAYER

Dear Jesus, the Bible tells about how You healed sick and disabled people. This morning, I pray for everyone who is sick or disabled. I ask You to heal them—not only their bodies, Lord, but also their minds. Give them comfort and make them strong. Pull close to You those who don't know You. Inspire them to accept You as their Savior. Amen.

EVENING DEVOTION

Then they cried out to the Lord in their trouble. And He saved them from their suffering. He sent His Word and healed them. And He saved them from the grave. Let them give thanks to the Lord for His loving-kindness and His great works to the children of men!
PSALM 107:19–21

The writer of today's psalm had firsthand experience of the love and saving power of God. This personal knowledge drove him to wish that others would praise God and know of His wonderful works as well. Does God's goodness to you inspire you to tell others about Him and cause you to work harder to let others know how great He is?

BEST INHERITANCE
(Acts 19:23–41)

MORNING PRAYER

Father God, there is only one way to You, and that's through Jesus. Some people believe they can get to heaven by being good or doing good things. But it doesn't work like that. You sent Jesus to save us from our sins. Accepting Him as Savior is the only way to receive Your gift of eternal life in heaven. Please open the eyes of those who don't get it. Help them to understand. Amen.

EVENING DEVOTION

Then David said to his son Solomon, "Be strong. Have strength of heart, and do it. Do not be afraid or troubled, for the Lord God, my God, is with you. He will not stop helping you. He will not leave you until all the work of the house of the Lord is finished."
1 CHRONICLES 28:20

In today's passage, David spoke to his son Solomon, encouraging him to be strong and courageous and to rely on God. David knew that his God would continue to be faithful to Solomon all the days of his life. Maybe you will have children one day and teach them to have a personal relationship with God. That is the best inheritance—a lasting gift—you can leave to your kids.

VALUE
(2 Chronicles 2)

MORNING PRAYER

God, Solomon chose people who didn't believe in God and lived in other nations to build the temple. Did Jewish builders wonder why they weren't chosen? You have a special way of assigning Your work. I'm amazed by the people You choose to do some of Your most important jobs. I wonder—what valuable assignments will You have for me in the future? I can't wait to find out. Lead the way, God. I'm ready. Amen.

EVENING DEVOTION

He pours anger on rulers. He makes them walk in the waste places where there is no path. But He lifts those in need out of their troubles. He makes their families grow like flocks.
PSALM 107:40–41

God doesn't do things the way the world does. While we celebrate the rich, beautiful, and powerful, He delights in the poor, lonely, and needy. It would do us good to see the world through His eyes and to value what He values.

ROOTED IN HOPE

(Acts 20:17–38)

MORNING PRAYER

Heavenly Father, Paul is a good example of a man who was humble, up-front, personal, and fair to everyone. He never failed to share the gospel with those he met. Help me to become a man like him. I want to share the good news about Jesus' gift of heaven with all my friends. I've failed at that in the past. Correct me so I'll do better next time. Thank You, God. Amen.

EVENING DEVOTION

"But in every city I have been, the Holy Spirit tells me that trouble and chains will be waiting for me there. But I am not worried about this. I do not think of my life as worth much, but I do want to finish the work the Lord Jesus gave me to do. My work is to preach the Good News of God's loving-favor."
ACTS 20:23–24

Paul knew that trouble, even prison, waited for him wherever he preached. Most of us would have given up. But not Paul! He wrote about facing it all with joy, even when he was threatened. The only reason for Paul's attitude was he knew God very well. His joy was entirely disconnected from his circumstances. Instead, it was rooted in his relationship with God and his hope for a life forever with Jesus.

AMONG US
(2 Chronicles 6:12–42)

MORNING PRAYER

Lord God, You are even bigger than all Your creation. I'm the smallest Who in Whoville and calling for help. You hear me! I want to praise You so powerfully that my words explode through the roof and spill into my neighborhood, into my city, and across the earth. Hear my praises join with those of other believers. You are our God! Our wonderful, amazing God. Amen.

EVENING DEVOTION

"But is it true that God will live with man on the earth? See, heaven and the highest heaven cannot hold You. How much less can this house hold You which I have built!"
2 CHRONICLES 6:18

Solomon was right when he said not even the highest heaven can contain God. Because of this, he wondered how God could ever live on the earth with humans. And yet God did live on the earth in the form of Jesus, a humble and self-sacrificing Man. And now God lives in us through His Holy Spirit. That He, Almighty God, decided to live among us and in us is a truth almost too incredible to imagine.

DAY 204

2 CHRONICLES 7:11–9:28
ACTS 21:15–32
PSALM 109:21–31

WISE DECISIONS
(Psalm 109:21–31)

Heavenly Father, I turn to You with all my decisions and requests for help. Where else would I go? You are good. Your love never fails. I'm weak, but in You, I find my strength. When I call on You for help, You are always there. You hear me. You bless me and lift me above my troubles. I thank You for the storms You've brought me through. I will praise You, God, forever. Amen.

The next day Paul took the men. He went through the religious worship of washing with them. They went into the house of God to tell when their religious worship of washing would be finished. Then the gift for each one of them would be given as an act of worship.
ACTS 21:26

In today's passage, Paul purified himself by washing according to Jewish custom. This was not something that he as a Christian needed to do. He participated in another culture's tradition solely for the sake of the gospel, believing that it would allow him to reach more people for Christ. How can you do the same today?

SEEKING
(Acts 22:14–16)

MORNING PRAYER

Dear God, sometimes I get so tired. The tasks You give me seem impossible, more than I'm ready for. I keep asking You for help. Maybe You are trying to tell me the time has come for me to stop asking and to start acting on what I know—getting right with You, obeying You, and doing my best. In Your perfect time, You will give me all the help I need. Amen.

EVENING DEVOTION

*And he did what was sinful, because he did
not follow the Lord with all his heart.*
2 CHRONICLES 12:14

Rehoboam slipped into sin because he did not prepare his heart to seek the Lord. What steps have you taken to prepare your heart to seek God? Do you have a regular devotional time? Do you faithfully attend church? Are you committed to reading and memorizing the Bible? If you don't act to seek and serve God, you risk slipping into sin, like Rehoboam did. Set your heart to seek God and you will find Him. He will reward you for seeking.

WINNING

(Acts 23:11)

MORNING PRAYER

Dear Jesus, teach me to follow Your will and to follow You willingly. When I read about Paul, I wonder if I could be as faithful and brave as he was. Paul followed Your will when he knew it meant going to prison or being put to death. I want to obey You and follow wherever You lead me, even if someday You send me on a dangerous mission, like You did Paul. Amen.

EVENING DEVOTION

"Now see, God is with us at our head. His religious leaders are ready to blow the horns, to sound the call to battle against you. O sons of Israel, do not fight against the Lord God of your fathers. For you cannot win."

2 CHRONICLES 13:12

Satan thought he could win when fighting against God, but Jesus defeated Satan and death when He offered His life on the cross. Satan wants you to turn away from God so you won't have eternal life in heaven. Jesus wants you to live forever. If you choose to fight against Jesus and follow your own will and not His, you will lose the battle. But if you choose to stand with Jesus, your Savior, you will always be on the winning side.

GOD IS AWARE
(2 Chronicles 17:7–10)

MORNING PRAYER

Heavenly Father, King Jehoshaphat sent out his best servants to teach Your Word to the people. Ben-hail, Shemaiah, and Elishama must have studied the scriptures carefully to be able to teach them. What they learned through Your Word must have changed their lives. And through these people, You changed their nation. Guide me to be like them. I want to encourage others and teach them about the Bible and You. Amen.

EVENING DEVOTION

*"For the eyes of the Lord move over all the earth
so that He may give strength to those whose whole
heart is given to Him. You have done a foolish
thing. So from now on you will have wars."*
2 CHRONICLES 16:9

Sometimes it might seem like God isn't doing much in the world or that He has given up on us because we've strayed so far from Him. But the truth is, God is always watching over the earth. He stands up for those whose hearts are His. He doesn't just stand by and watch. God is already aware of what's happening in your life. So whenever you have a need, call on Him. He's ready to help.

COURAGE TO SPEAK

(Psalm 112)

MORNING PRAYER

Before I pray for Your blessings, Lord, I ask You to make me a better person. Grow my compassion and generosity. Lead me nearer to You so I will feel stronger and more secure. I want to respect You more deeply and find increased joy in knowing You. Jesus, I praise You! You've blessed me in so many wonderful ways. Add to my blessings today as I go about my work. Amen.

EVENING DEVOTION

The king of Israel said to him, "There is yet one man whom we may ask of the Lord. But I hate him. For he never tells me anything good, only bad. He is Micaiah, the son of Imla." But Jehoshaphat said, "You should not say that."
2 CHRONICLES 18:7

Micaiah was faithful in relaying messages from God. The king of Israel hated him because Micaiah never told the king what he wanted to hear. Maybe you've found yourself in a similar situation: when you speak about God and the Bible, the person listening doesn't want to hear what you have to say. Be courageous. Don't be afraid to talk about God and His Word. What matters most is what God thinks of you, not how others receive what you say.

JUST PRAISE
(2 Chronicles 20:25)

MORNING PRAYER

Dear God, sometimes I make some unhealthy choices. Forgive me! You provide me with every good thing I need, so why do I sometimes choose what's bad? I have to stay focused on You and choose more wisely. Open my eyes to Your ways. Keep me on a straight path. I want every choice I make to please You. Amen.

EVENING DEVOTION

Then he said, "O Lord, the God of our fathers, are You not God in heaven? Do You not rule over all the nations? Power and strength are in Your hand, so that no one is able to stand against You. O our God, did You not make the people of this land leave so that Your people Israel could have it and give it to the children of Your friend Abraham forever?"
2 CHRONICLES 20:6–7

When you pray, remember and rely on God's promises in the Bible. Jehoshaphat was aware of God's past work and His faithfulness. Because he knew God keeps His promises, Jehoshaphat went into battle praising God (2 Chronicles 20:21). When you face your own battles, face them with praise like Jehoshaphat did. You have nothing to be afraid of.

A GOOD LIFE
(2 Chronicles 22–23)

MORNING PRAYER

Lord God, 2 Chronicles 22–23: what a story! One woman causes a mess for the kingdom and another acts with great love, bravely sweeping a baby straight out of the royal nursery to safety. As much as I want to be brave and wise like Jehoshabeath, at times I think I act selfishly like Athaliah. Forgive me. Keep me from wanting what others have. Take any jealous thoughts from my mind and heart. Amen.

EVENING DEVOTION

Paul said, "My prayer to God is that you and
all who hear me today would be a Christian
as I am, only not have these chains!"
ACTS 26:29

It's easy to dwell on the things in your life that aren't going well. No matter what's going on, remember that you're blessed. Why? Because you have a solid relationship with Jesus. That alone is reason to say, "I have a good life!" Paul knew how blessed he was, and he wished others had the kind of loving and personal relationship he had with his Savior. Paul decided he had a truly good life even when he was suffering and chained in prison.

GOOD MENTORS
(Psalm 115:1–10)

MORNING PRAYER

Father God, I want everything I do to bring You honor. I want others to see You through me when I tell them of all the wonderful things You've done for me: how You've given me strength when I felt weak and calmed me when I felt afraid. I want them to know of Your love, power, and faithfulness. Make me like a mirror, God, that reflects only You. Amen.

EVENING DEVOTION

*But after the death of Jehoiada, the leaders
of Judah came and bowed down in front of
the king. And the king listened to them.*
2 CHRONICLES 24:17

Did you know you can be a mentor—someone who helps another person by teaching or giving advice? Maybe you could mentor a younger sibling or a kid in your neighborhood or school. You might be able to help him with his schoolwork, show him how to play a sport, or teach him something new. Do you have advice to share, something that might make a difficult situation easier? You especially can mentor someone to follow Jesus. Think about it: Has an older person been a mentor to you?

THE COURSE GOD SETS
(Acts 27:21–41)

MORNING PRAYER

Lord God, Paul was shipwrecked, and I can imagine the shipwrecks in my own life. Sometimes I feel like I'm bailing water; other times I feel like abandoning ship. But I'm not alone! You are with me, guiding me through the storm. I turn to You with faith that You'll save me. God, I pray for others who are sailing a stormy sea. Be with them. Help them. Keep them safe and sound. Amen.

EVENING DEVOTION

*"So take hope, men. I believe my God
will do what He has told me."*
ACTS 27:25

Paul understood that God had a plan for him, and he knew God would keep him on course until His plan was fulfilled. Paul's faith in God's plan was rock solid. He believed God had given him a purpose, and he was ready and willing for God to use him. Not even a shipwreck could alter the course God had set for him. Is your faith that rock solid?

A BEAUTIFUL MESSAGE

(2 Chronicles 29:1–9)

MORNING PRAYER

Dear God, King Hezekiah did what he knew was right. He got the people to turn from their false gods and sinful ways. He literally cleaned out the temple and made it like new. Sometimes I need to do that too. I need a good cleaning inside to get rid of the sin and all those things I've made more important than You. God, clean my heart and mind. Make me beautiful in Your sight. Amen.

EVENING DEVOTION

"We would like to hear from you what you believe. As for this new religion, all we know is that everyone is talking against it."
ACTS 28:22

The message of salvation—the good news that Jesus died for our sins and made a way for us to live in heaven—is the most powerful message ever heard. Yet throughout history, people have spoken against it, saying it isn't true. Or they change the message to say salvation has to be earned. Or they insist there are other ways to get to heaven. Isn't it sad that people put up so much resistance to such a powerful and simple message?

NOT THE END
(Romans 1:7–10)

MORNING PRAYER

Dear Jesus, what do my friends, classmates, neighbors, even strangers I meet think of me? Do my words, texts, and actions make them think of You? I pray that what people think of me will remind them of You. I hope they will want what I have—forgiveness of sins and a forever relationship with You. Thank You for helping me to be the best I can be. Amen.

EVENING DEVOTION

The death of His holy ones is of great worth in the eyes of the Lord.
PSALM 116:15

People who put their trust in Jesus never die. Death isn't the end for them; it's the beginning of an incredible new life in heaven. While we miss people when they die, we should remember they are living a life that never ends. If you believe in Jesus, your life won't end either. Your body will die, but *you* will move to your new home where you'll be with the family and friends who went before you—and that's something to celebrate!

HEAVENLY ARMY

(Psalm 117)

MORNING PRAYER

Dear God, I wonder what it would sound like to hear all the Christians on earth praising You together. What does it sound like in heaven when the angels sing songs of praise? As I pray this morning, my prayer joins thousands, maybe millions, of other prayers happening right now. What does that sound like to You? Is it music to Your ears? Lord God, I praise You! Amen.

EVENING DEVOTION

"Be strong and have strength of heart. Do not be afraid or troubled because of the king of Assyria and all those who are with him. For the One with us is greater than the one with him. He has only man with him. But we have the Lord our God with us, to help us and to fight our battles." And the people trusted the words of Hezekiah king of Judah.
2 Chronicles 32:7–8

What a powerful and inspiring speech from King Hezekiah in today's passage. The terrifying Assyrian army was threatening God's people. But instead of giving in to fear, Hezekiah told them to rely on God. No matter how big a problem you face, no matter how scary it is, remember that God and His army are fighting for you—and no army is bigger or more powerful than His.

THE MAKER
(Psalm 118:1–18)

MORNING PRAYER

Dear God, each morning I wake up ready to face the day with You by my side. What You have to give me never runs out. If I need more strength, You have plenty to offer me. If I need more courage, plenty of that is waiting too. Comfort? Love? Forgiveness? It's all there for the taking. You never let me down. You are always faithful. You meet all my needs all the time. Thank You, God! I love You. Amen.

EVENING DEVOTION

The people who are not Jews do not have the Law. When they do what the Law tells them to do, even if they do not have the Law, it shows they know what they should do. They show that what the Law wants them to do is written in their hearts. Their own hearts tell them if they are guilty.

ROMANS 2:14–15

No matter how hard people may fight against the idea of a Creator, their conscience proves He exists. God sets a moral standard in our hearts, a feeling of right over wrong. When we choose sin, we experience a nagging feeling of guilt. Some people try to push down those negative feelings and pretend God doesn't see or care. But He does. God wants people to admit their sins, come to Him for forgiveness, and be saved through belief and trust in Jesus.

THE SAME
(Romans 3:1–26)

MORNING PRAYER

God, You amaze me. Heaven, where You are, seems like a different place than earth. Yet while You are there, You are also here with me through the Holy Spirit! Thanks to Jesus, I am free from my sins, and someday I will spend eternity with You. For now, I will live my life with the Holy Spirit as my guide. Amazing! Amen.

EVENING DEVOTION

Men become right with God by putting their trust in Jesus Christ. God will accept men if they come this way. All men are the same to God. For all men have sinned and have missed the shining-greatness of God.
ROMANS 3:22–23

Standing before God, we will all be judged equally. All of us have sinned and are in need of His forgiveness. None of us can live up to His standards on our own. In God's eyes, there is no special treatment because of skin color, popularity, physical ability, or appearance. And if God sees us as equal, that's how we need to see each other. We are all humans, created by Him with differences that reflect His creativity and wisdom—not one of us is better than another.

2 CHRONICLES 35:20–36:23
ROMANS 3:27–4:25
PSALM 118:24–29

TODAY IS THE DAY
(Psalm 118:24)

MORNING PRAYER

Heavenly Father, what better day than today to praise You? This is the day You have made, and I give it back to You as an offering. I will do my best to make this a day when You are pleased with all I do. Every minute is a new beginning, and I want to make the most of my time, serving You in every way I can. Amen.

EVENING DEVOTION

This is the day that the Lord has made. Let us be full of joy and be glad in it.
PSALM 118:24

"This is the day that the Lord has made. Let us be full of joy and be glad in it." This is a choice we can make every morning: God has made today, so I will be glad. On days when it's hard to find joy in anything, you can be joyful that God has given you another new day with new things to do and new blessings from Him. He has planned out this day for you. Be glad for every new day.

TRUE PEACE
(Romans 5:1–5)

MORNING PRAYER

God, thank You for all the ways hope works in my life. When things don't go my way, I have hope because I know You will always help me. Hope fills me with Your love because I know You care for me and will keep me safe. I have hope because so many times You have kept me from trouble. Today, I will tell others of the hope I have in You. Amen.

EVENING DEVOTION

Now that we have been made right with God by putting our trust in Him, we have peace with Him. It is because of what our Lord Jesus Christ did for us. By putting our trust in God, He has given us His loving-favor and has received us. We are happy for the hope we have of sharing the shining-greatness of God.
ROMANS 5:1–2

Where does your peace come from? Not from relationships, your healthy body, or any of your stuff. It comes from being made perfect before God. Someday you will stand before Him in His kingdom, perfect because of Jesus. True peace comes from knowing that Jesus has saved you from sin and promised you a place in heaven.

MEMORIZING GOD'S WORD
(Romans 6)

MORNING PRAYER

Lord Jesus, help me to make wise choices today—choices that please You. Remind me of the Bible verses I've memorized, especially those that have taught me right from wrong. If I feel tired or discouraged today, keep me from choosing sin. Refresh me and make me feel new so I can spend today doing only what's pleasing in Your sight. Amen.

EVENING DEVOTION

*Your Word have I hid in my heart, that
I may not sin against You.*
PSALM 119:11

Memorizing God's Word is important. Having scripture verses in your heart and mind gives you power to avoid sin. Scripture guides you toward God's will. When you feel like doing something you know is wrong, quote scripture to yourself. God's Word is the best weapon you have against sin. Add scripture to your memory bank. Hide God's Word in your heart and keep it ready all the time for whatever needs you have.

GOD IS IN CONTROL
(Ezra 6)

MORNING PRAYER

Dear God, my prayer this morning is for leaders everywhere—world leaders and those who lead my country and community. I pray for church leaders and leaders in my school. Be near to them. Guide them. Give them wisdom to make decisions that please You. Most of all, God, I pray that each one will come to know and recognize You, like Darius did. Amen.

EVENING DEVOTION

"Also, I am making it known what you are to do for these leaders of Judah for the building of this house of God. All of it is to be paid for from the king's money out of the taxes from the lands on the other side of the River. And waste no time to get it to them."
EZRA 6:8

Stories in the books of Ezra and Nehemiah demonstrate how God is in control no matter how out of control a situation may seem. The people's mission to rebuild the house of God was constantly facing a shutdown. In today's passage, King Darius (the ruler of an enemy nation that had captured God's people) not only allowed them to continue their work but even assisted them with their project. God has never lost control. He is always, and always will be, in charge.

DAY 222

EZRA 7:27–9:4
ROMANS 8:1–27
PSALM 119:33–40

WHAT GOD HAS DONE

(Ezra 8:21–23)

MORNING PRAYER

Mighty God, Ezra was awesome! He refused to ask for help because he had bragged that You were His help in all situations. If ever I doubt what You can do, remind me of Ezra. Every day, You watch over me and help me. Thank You, God, for being my help. And thank You also for the people You send to help me. I often forget that they are like Your angels in disguise. Amen.

EVENING DEVOTION

*Now, because of this, those who belong to Christ
will not suffer the punishment of sin.*
ROMANS 8:1

Do you understand that Jesus made it possible for you to not be punished for your sins? If you've accepted Jesus as your Savior, He already paid the price for any wrong thing you do on the earth. Of course, God wants you to do your best to live a life that is pleasing to Him. But when you mess up—and you will!—know that God won't leave you or turn against you. He extends His forgiveness to you, free for the taking.

POWER OVER SIN

(Psalm 119:41–64)

MORNING PRAYER

Heavenly Father, Your forgiveness requires only that I tell You about my sins and try to do better. As hard as I try, I can never be perfect—not until that day when You make me perfect in heaven. I'm grateful for Your never-ending forgiveness and that each day You love me so much that You give me a fresh start. Help me today to do my best. Amen.

EVENING DEVOTION

*But we have power over all these things
through Jesus Who loves us so much.*
ROMANS 8:37

Memorize Romans 8:37. Then anytime you feel you're losing a battle with sin, you will be reminded that Jesus paid the price and gave you power over sin. Absolutely nothing has the power to separate you from His love. Even when you mess up and do something you know would displease Him, God continues to love you. Be sure of this: His love will be with you forever.

DO THIS: PRAY!

(Romans 9:18)

MORNING PRAYER

Father God, I'm so grateful You've welcomed me into Your family. I'm grateful too for my family members and friends who call Jesus their Savior. This morning, I pray for those who don't know You. They don't know what they're missing, God—how life is so much better when You live inside a person's heart. Lead them to accept You and Your gift of eternal life. Amen.

EVENING DEVOTION

Then the king said to me, "What are you asking for?" So I prayed to the God of heaven.

NEHEMIAH 2:4

Nehemiah was standing in the courts of the king, and the king asked him what he wanted. What would be your first response? Nehemiah's reaction was to pray. Even in the middle of the king's court, Nehemiah's prayers continued. Through prayer, he was constantly in the court of his heavenly King. Prayer is too often a second or third choice for us. Try to be more like Nehemiah so that your natural first response is to pray.

LIFE'S HARD QUESTIONS

(Psalm 119:73–80)

MORNING PRAYER

Lord, I love reading the Bible and learning about Your power. I find comfort in Your promises and the ways You care for me. Your Word changes me. It asks hard questions and reminds me of areas of my life in which I need to grow. The more I understand Your Word, the more prepared I am to share it with others. Please continue to use the Bible to teach me. Amen.

EVENING DEVOTION

Who are you to talk back to God? A pot being made from clay does not talk to the man making it and say, "Why did you make me like this?"
ROMANS 9:20

Romans 9:20 provides a reply to the many times we doubt God's work: Who are we to question God? His thoughts, ways, wisdom, and knowledge are so far above ours that we can't begin to understand them. Remembering how small we are compared to God and trusting in His wisdom and love will help us greatly when we face hard questions.

INNER CONVERSATION

(Nehemiah 6:9)

MORNING PRAYER

God, if someone makes fun of me or tells me I'm not smart, talented, or strong enough to do something, give me strength. When I'm nervous or afraid to start a job, make me steady and give my actions purpose. When I doubt my work is worth the effort or time, open my eyes to all the possibilities and bring me help if I need it. And when I succeed, I will give all the praise to You. Amen.

EVENING DEVOTION

For they all wanted to make us afraid, thinking, "Their hands will become weak and the work will not be done." But now, O God, strengthen my hands.
NEHEMIAH 6:9

Nehemiah 6:9 is a quick prayer Nehemiah spoke to God when he was afraid—"O God, strengthen my hands." We can imagine this was just one of many quick prayers Nehemiah prayed. He was always talking with God and tapping into God's power. Make Nehemiah a role model for your prayer life. Get in the habit of talking with God throughout your day.

DELIGHT IN GOD'S WORD

(Romans 10:14–15)

MORNING PRAYER

Lord Jesus, people who haven't heard of You can't call on You. I forget that some people in the world don't even know Your name. Is there some way I can reach them? Maybe I can help missionaries through my church. Give me some ideas, Lord. I want people all over the world not only to know Your name but also to accept You as their Savior. Amen.

EVENING DEVOTION

*I would have been lost in my troubles if
Your Law had not been my joy.*
PSALM 119:92

David had learned to delight in the Word of God. It became his everything. In today's passage, he says reading the Bible, finding joy in its words, was the reason he could overcome any kind of trouble. God's Word will do the same for you. It will help you through all kinds of circumstances and lead you into a stronger relationship with God. Don't miss out on the opportunity to delight in the Lord. Read your Bible every day.

DAY 228

NEHEMIAH 9:6–10:27
ROMANS 11:25–12:8
PSALM 119:105–120

LIGHT TO YOUR PATH
(Nehemiah 9:6–37)

MORNING PRAYER

Lord God, You are God of the highest heaven, God of the depths of the sea, and God to the far ends of the universe, so how is it that You see me? Compared with You, I'm tiny, like a grain of sand, and my troubles are like specks of dust. Yet You care about me and all my concerns, great and small. God, I love You and I praise You. Amen.

EVENING DEVOTION

Your Word is a lamp to my feet and a light to my path.
PSALM 119:105

The psalmist, possibly David, said God's Word was a lamp to his feet and a light to his path. If you need direction in your life, go to God's Word—the Bible. God has already provided you with all the light you need to navigate the path to your future. Dig into the Bible and learn all you can from it. In turn, God will use His Word to light your way.

PRIDE
(Romans 12:20–21)

MORNING PRAYER

Lord Jesus, Romans 12:20 says, "If the one who hates you is hungry, feed him. If he is thirsty, give him water. If you do that, you will be making him more ashamed of himself." I need to remember that. When people are against me, I usually want to be against them. But that's giving in to sin. Responding with kindness is Your advice, and I'll do my best to follow it. Amen.

EVENING DEVOTION

Live in peace with each other. Do not act or think with pride. Be happy to be with poor people. Keep yourself from thinking you are so wise.
ROMANS 12:16

Do you know a lot about something? Does that knowledge make you feel smarter or better than someone else? A big ego and a conceited attitude aren't pleasing to God. Think about Jesus. He was God who came to earth in a human body. He had knowledge of the entire universe, and still, He humbled Himself to live among His people. If you know a lot about something, instead of telling others about how much you know, put your knowledge to good use in serving God.

GOD'S HEART
(Psalm 119:129–136)

MORNING PRAYER

Jesus, Your wonderful words in the Bible are like warm sunlight. They show me the path to take, and they keep me from stumbling into sin. And when I do sin, You still love me. You forgive me and wash away my sin so I can start fresh again. If others try to lead me astray, I hear You guiding me back to You. Thank You, Jesus, for Your words! Amen.

EVENING DEVOTION

Your Laws are wonderful, and so I obey them.
PSALM 119:129

In Psalm 119, we see the great love David had for God's Word. He was someone who had carefully studied God's laws and promises. It's no wonder David was a man who reflected God's own heart. God's heart is open to us in His Word. We come to know Him more fully, like David did, every time we read the Bible.

OVERFLOW WITH HOPE

(Romans 14:13–15:13)

MORNING PRAYER

God, this morning I join in with other Christians, asking You to fill the world with joy and peace. Help us to come together, even if our worship practices look a little different from place to place. We are all Yours. Teach us not to judge each other but instead to live in a way that leads us to build each other up and work together to serve You. Amen.

EVENING DEVOTION

Our hope comes from God. May He fill you with joy and peace because of your trust in Him. May your hope grow stronger by the power of the Holy Spirit.
ROMANS 15:13

Hope, as described in the Bible, isn't the same as a wish that might happen. Instead, it's faith that something is sure to happen. God is the God of hope because without His work and promises, there would be nothing to have faith in and nothing we could be sure of. Remember Paul's words in Romans 15:13. Ask God to fill you with joy and peace so your heart will overflow with hope through the Holy Spirit.

FOR SUCH A TIME AS THIS
(Psalm 119:165)

MORNING PRAYER

Dear Lord, some days I just want peace. There are lots of days when things seem crazy busy or messed up. Please give me today as a day of peace. I'm weak without You. Make me strong. Fill my heart with You today, and give me peace in everything I do. Remind me all day of Your words. Comfort me, guide me, and keep me focused on You. Amen.

EVENING DEVOTION

"For if you keep quiet at this time, help will come to the Jews from another place. But you and your father's house will be destroyed. Who knows if you have not become queen for such a time as this?"
ESTHER 4:14

Did you know there's no reference to God in the book of Esther? Still, we see evidence of Him throughout the whole story. You might not notice when God is working out His will for You, but you can be sure He is present and working on your behalf. Just like Esther, God has you exactly where He wants you. You are where you should be for a very specific reason. . ."for such a time as this."

COMMITMENT
(Esther 8)

MORNING PRAYER

Dear God, You gave Mordecai and Esther all the tools they needed to solve their problem—but they had to use them! You do the same for me: You give me wisdom, courage, and strength to get through my problems, but I have to use those tools. Sometimes I think You'll do it all for me. Now I understand that I have to commit to do the work. Please help me to grow into a man who is wise like Mordecai was wise. And help me to be brave like Esther was. Amen.

EVENING DEVOTION

*May Your hand be ready to help me,
for I have chosen Your Law.*
PSALM 119:173

David said he had chosen to follow God's laws. Wanting to know and follow God's Word is a choice and a commitment. Sometimes we get so caught up in doing what we want that obedience to God slides. Make a commitment every day to read, memorize, and think about God's Word. God will reward your commitment with His blessings.

DAY 234

ESTHER 9–10
ROMANS 16
PSALMS 120–122

PURSUE GOD
(Psalm 121)

MORNING PRAYER

Heavenly Father, Your words give me courage and comfort. Stand guard over me today. Help me to do what is good, and keep me from falling into sin. I'm grateful that You are with me, watching over me from the time I leave this morning until the time I come home—always! With Your greatness, lead me through this day. Amen.

EVENING DEVOTION

Everyone knows you have obeyed the teaching you received. I am happy with you because of this. But I want you to be wise about good things and pure about sinful things.
ROMANS 16:19

In today's culture, there seems to be more evil around us than good. Paul gives us simple advice: don't pursue evil. Leave it alone. Don't go after things that tear down, that promote violence or abuse, or that are simply worthless. Instead, follow only what's good, lovely, and valuable. Read the Bible and become an expert in right living. Be wise in what's good, and follow Paul's clear and simple advice to avoid evil.

GIVE AND TAKE AWAY
(Job 1:21)

MORNING PRAYER

Father God, Job brought his feelings to you. He kept his faith in You strong. He thanked You for the ways You had blessed him, and he stayed focused on You instead of his troubles. You had allowed so much to be taken from Job. Yet he held on to his faith in You. When the world seems to be crashing down around me, help me to have the same wisdom and faith as Job. Amen.

EVENING DEVOTION

He said, "Without clothing I was born from my mother, and without clothing I will return. The Lord gave and the Lord has taken away. Praise the name of the Lord."
JOB 1:21

Job understood that God was wiser than he could ever be, and if God could give blessings, He also had every right to take them away. Job understood that he came into the world with nothing and could take nothing with him into eternal life. He understood that he had a loose hold on his earthly possessions and relationships. Job chose to honor the Lord even in the middle of his terrible suffering.

FOR HIS PURPOSE

(Job 5:15–16)

MORNING PRAYER

Heavenly Father, I'm thankful for Job's example. His faith in You remained strong. When he had almost nothing left, he stayed committed to You. He knew You still cared for him when he was poor and needy. This morning, I pray for the poor. Bless them, God, and meet their needs. Rescue them from their troubles. Show me what I can do today to help You bless the lives of others. Amen.

EVENING DEVOTION

*But God has chosen what the world calls foolish
to shame the wise. He has chosen what the
world calls weak to shame what is strong.*

1 CORINTHIANS 1:27

God uses the weak, the broken, and even the foolish things of the world for His purposes. We see this all throughout scripture. Just as a piece of pottery can let light through only if it has cracks, God's light shines more clearly through those who don't have it all together. When God chooses to use us for His kingdom, our brokenness and weakness are what allow His power to become visible to those around us.

THE CROSS
(1 Corinthians 3:10–16)

MORNING PRAYER

Lord Jesus, through Your death on the cross, You opened up a way for me to enter God's kingdom. You gave me a pure heart, and not only that—You came to live in my heart forever. You live inside me now. Work within me. Change my thoughts to be more like Your thoughts. Make me more like You. Fill me up with You, Jesus. I want more of You every day. Amen.

EVENING DEVOTION

"Yes, I know this is true. But how can a man be right and good before God? If one wished to argue with Him, he would not be able to answer one out of a thousand of His questions."
JOB 9:2–3

Job asked an important question: How can someone be right with God when he has nothing of value to offer? Since Job didn't have the blessing of knowing what Jesus would do on the cross (he lived long before that event), standing before God seemed hopeless for Job based on what he had to give. We have the huge blessing of being saved from our sin through our trust in Jesus. He makes us right with God even though we have nothing of value to offer.

BLAMELESS
(Job 11:18)

MORNING PRAYER

God, I feel secure in Your never-failing love. Thank You for giving me hope. When I can face obstacles with optimism, it's because of the hope You give me. You remind me that You are my safety net. You hold me tight and secure. I have peace knowing You are the one guiding me. With You, I have everything I need to face whatever comes my way. Thank You, God. I praise You! Amen.

EVENING DEVOTION

As for me, my heart tells me I am not guilty of anything. But that does not prove I am free from guilt. It is the Lord Who looks into my life and says what is wrong.
1 CORINTHIANS 4:4

In his heart, Paul knew he wasn't guilty of anything. Can you say the same about yourself? Do you try to live your life in such a way that you can have a clear, guiltless conscience before God? You can never achieve perfection on your own, so stop trying. Jesus has already made you guilt-free through His death on the cross. Live as best as you can to please God and to stay free of guilt. You are already blameless in God's eyes.

BRIGHTEST
(Psalm 130)

MORNING PRAYER

Heavenly Father, I'm looking forward to this day. I wonder what You have waiting for me. Like the psalm writer said, I'm waiting for You like someone in the night waiting for morning. When the sun came up this morning, I thought of You shining Your light on the world—and on me. You have never disappointed me. You always deliver what You've promised. I'm ready for today. Let's go! Amen.

EVENING DEVOTION

*I do not write these things to shame you. I am
doing this to help you know what you should do.
You are my much-loved children. . . . So I ask you
with all my heart to follow the way I live.*
1 CORINTHIANS 4:14, 16

In today's verse, Paul tells the Corinthians not to be fooled into sinning when they hang out with nonbelievers. Paul didn't tell them never to be around those who don't believe in Jesus. In fact, he actually said that as Christians, we should be getting to know everyone. Never being with nonbelievers means we would miss out on the most important reason for being a Christian—sharing the best news ever about Jesus' wonderful gift of salvation.

DAY 240

JOB 17–20
1 CORINTHIANS 6
PSALM 131

CHILD-LIKE TRUST
(Psalm 131)

MORNING PRAYER

Heavenly Father, I want to be like the person in this psalm, feeling content, knowing that You think I'm special and You love me. I want to feel You near me always, safe and confident, trusting that You are in control. God, keep me from worrying about things, especially those I can't do anything about. Every day I want to know You better and become more like You. Amen.

EVENING DEVOTION

"But as for me, I know that the One Who bought me and made me free from sin lives, and that He will stand upon the earth in the end. Even after my skin is destroyed, yet in my flesh I will see God."
JOB 19:25–26

Job had a clear vision of God coming to earth to make things right again. Job knew that one day his body would live again. He knew that one day the Messiah—who we know to be Jesus—would stand on the earth. In the middle of Job's suffering, God comforted him with that vision. It wasn't the end for Job—or for any other person who believes. Jesus is coming, and He will make everything right.

STRONGER
(1 Corinthians 7:1–16)

MORNING PRAYER

Dear God, I wonder if it's Your plan for me, when the time is right, to get married. It's hard to imagine becoming a husband and a dad with children of my own, but maybe that's what you want for me. Are you leading me to meet my future wife? Or maybe Your plan is for me to stay single. In that case, I trust that You'll have some wonderful experiences waiting for me. Where will You lead me? I can't wait to know. Amen.

EVENING DEVOTION

*"But He knows the way that I take. When He
has tried me, I will come out as gold."*
JOB 23:10

Job understood suffering. He understood God was polishing him the way you would polish a dirty piece of priceless gold. Often it's the really hard times in life that give us the greatest strength. If we hold tightly to God in hard times, our faith grows stronger. He will bring us through our troubles, and we'll come out like a glittering piece of gold, worth the process of polishing.

SPENDING TIME
(Job 26:13–14)

MORNING PRAYER

Lord God, every day I see You in nature—in the sunrise, the plants, the animals, the moon, and the stars. What I see is just the edge of Your wonderful and amazing creation. Open my eyes today to even more of Your creation. You are present everywhere. Forgive me when I get so wrapped up in my own little world that I fail to see You in the big picture. Amen.

EVENING DEVOTION

See, how good and how pleasing it is for brothers to live together as one!
PSALM 133:1

It is good and pleasing for God's people to live together in unity. Relationships are hard. People will disagree and cause issues. But having relationships with other believers is precious enough that we should be doing our best to live in peace and unity with other Christians as much as possible. God has placed us in relationships so we can enjoy each other and help each other. Don't miss out on the value of spending time with His people.

KNOWLEDGE
(Psalm 135)

MORNING PRAYER

I praise You, Lord. I praise You at church and also in my quiet time alone with You at home. I praise You with other Christians all over the world. We praise You because we know who You are—You are great, greater than anyone or anything else. I want to learn from others about their experiences of knowing You. Lead me to other Christians and let me hear their stories. Amen.

EVENING DEVOTION

The person who thinks he knows all the answers still has a lot to learn. But if he loves God, he is known by God also.
1 CORINTHIANS 8:2–3

God is so great that we can know only a little about Him. The rest is beyond our understanding. It's true that the more we learn, the more we realize how little we know about our Creator. Make it your goal to find out as much as you can about Him. Though your knowledge of God will always be limited, He knows you perfectly. He knows you better than you will ever know yourself.

LOVING-KINDNESS FOREVER

(Job 31:35)

MORNING PRAYER

Almighty God, Job cried out for You to hear him. You did hear him, and You hear me too. You hear all of us when we cry out Your name. If someone wrongly accuses me, I can count on You to set things right. Because You have taken away my sin, You will toss out any complaint against me. Even when I don't deserve it, You will save me. Amen.

EVENING DEVOTION

*Give thanks to the Lord, for He is good, for
His loving-kindness lasts forever.*
PSALM 136:1

The words "for His loving-kindness lasts forever" appear more than two dozen times in Psalm 136. Each verse ends with that phrase, like a period. How many times recently could your circumstances have ended with those words? God's loving-kindness, His mercy, is woven throughout our days in both small and life-changing ways. And His loving-kindness will last forever, even into our lives in heaven.

RICHES OF THE GOSPEL

(1 Corinthians 10:12–13)

MORNING PRAYER

God, I'm beginning to see that the temptations I face—those things I might do that displease You—are more common than I thought. When I talk with my friends, I see that they have the same struggles. Often we are challenged to choose right from wrong. Your Word, the Bible, can help us make right choices. Today, I pray for myself and my friends that we will choose what is right. Amen.

EVENING DEVOTION

Some are weak. I have become weak so I might lead them to Christ. I have become like every person so in every way I might lead some to Christ. Everything I do, I do to get the Good News to men. I want to have a part in this work.
1 CORINTHIANS 9:22–23

Paul's goal was to reach as many people as he could to tell them about Jesus. What Paul wanted and needed no longer mattered. Paul was on a mission; his only purpose was to share the gospel, the good news that Jesus came to save us from sin. Paul sacrificed his own wants and riches—he made himself "weak"—so he could share the riches people find when they put their trust in the Lord.

GOOD CHOICES
(1 Corinthians 10:31)

MORNING PRAYER

Lord God, when I have to make a choice, remind me to ask myself, *Is the choice I want to make pleasing to God? Will it help to bring me or someone else nearer to Him?* I sometimes forget and make wrong choices. Forgive me. I want everything I do to please You and to be a reflection of Your goodness. I want to live to honor You and build up those around me. Amen.

EVENING DEVOTION

"Where were you when I began building the earth? Tell Me, if you have understanding."
JOB 38:4

When God speaks back to Job, His words are so powerful that they terrify Job and humble him. They make Job realize just how insignificant he is. Imagine being there, seeing and hearing the power of God. How could we ever begin to think we know better than Him? Were we there when He created the earth? Do we hold the universe together from day to day? Too often, we forget how magnificent God is and dare to think that our will is better than His.

READ. . .AND PRAY
(Job 42:1–6)

MORNING PRAYER

God, I need to remind myself that You are God, and I am not. Sometimes I do what I want, thinking it's what's best for me when You have a better plan. When I think of how often I disobey You, I feel ashamed. I see how small and weak I am compared to You. Keep reminding me that You are the God of the universe and I should put all my trust in You. Amen.

EVENING DEVOTION

"I know that You can do all things. Nothing can put a stop to Your plans. 'Who is this that hides words of wisdom without much learning?' I have said things that I did not understand, things too great for me, which I did not know."
JOB 42:2–3

When Job heard God speak, he responded with humility and praise. He knew his life would never be the same. God had put Job in his place—had spoken directly to him. Imagine how your life would change after you heard God speak to you. Think about this: every day God does speak to you through His words in the Bible. You hear His words in your heart when you pray. Doesn't that make you feel like Job, humble and wanting to praise Him?

DAY 248

ECCLESIASTES 1:1–3:15
1 CORINTHIANS 12:1–26
PSALM 139:1–6

OVER THE SUN
(Psalm 139:1–6)

MORNING PRAYER

Father, You keep a record of everything I do. You would be the perfect expert witness in a trial, explaining where I was, what I was doing, and why. I can't hide from You. You see everything I do and hear everything I say. I love that You care so much about me. I am just a tiny speck in the universe, and yet You love me. Thank You, God! I love You too. Amen.

EVENING DEVOTION

"It is of no use," says the Preacher. "It is of no use! All is for nothing." What does a man get for all his work which he does under the sun?
ECCLESIASTES 1:2–3

Ecclesiastes clearly describes life apart from God—life "under the sun." Anything we do apart from God's purposes is all for nothing. It's of no use. Ecclesiastes 3:11 says God has put thoughts of forever in our minds. There is more to living than just this life. We have the promise of forever in heaven if we put our trust in Jesus. To find contentment and happiness in this life, we need to live with our thoughts focused "over the sun."

THE LOVE GOD HAS FOR YOU

(Ecclesiastes 5:1–7)

MORNING PRAYER

When I pray, Lord, remind me to listen. Instead of just talking at You, I want to learn from You. Give me the strength to obey You when I'm tempted to disobey. Instead of accepting Your forgiveness and moving on, I want to remember the price Jesus paid for me to be forgiven. Your ways are higher than my ways, Lord. Teach me Your ways. Teach me to listen to and follow You. Amen.

EVENING DEVOTION

*Your eyes saw me before I was put together.
And all the days of my life were written in Your
book before any of them came to be.*
PSALM 139:16

God knew you before you were born, before anyone else was even aware of you. Before the first beat of your heart, God planned out a life for you, a journey you and He would take together. The careful thought He put into planning your life means you are of great value to Him. The opinions people have of you are nothing compared to the deep love God has for you.

LIGHT IN THE DARKNESS
(Psalm 139:23–24)

MORNING PRAYER

Lord Jesus, You know me better than I know myself. You know what's in my heart. You hold my worried thoughts in the palm of Your hand. You know when I do what's right, and You know when I sin. Help me to understand myself better. Open my eyes to things that displease You, things of which I'm unaware. I want to follow the path You've set for me and go wherever You lead. Amen.

EVENING DEVOTION

Whatever your hand finds to do, do it with all your strength. For there is no work or planning or learning or wisdom in the place of the dead where you are going.
ECCLESIASTES 9:10

While you live on earth, God gives you work to do for Him: to speak about Him to others and to help people, to comfort them and show them God's love, to become a man who treats others the way Jesus would. God wants you to make the most of your time on earth and to enjoy being His friend. Remember, you are working for God. Be a reflection of Him, shining His light in the darkness.

DAY 251

FOR OTHERS,
FOR THE KINGDOM
(1 Corinthians 14:40)

MORNING PRAYER

God, I learn an important lesson from 1 Corinthians 14:40. Paul said, "All things should be done in the right way, one after the other." The right way is always Your way. I'm beginning to understand that when I do what's right, it isn't just good for me—it's good for everyone around me. When others see me doing what's right, I'm setting an example. They might choose to do what's right because of me. Amen.

EVENING DEVOTION

The last word, after all has been heard, is: Honor God and obey His Laws. This is all that every person must do. For God will judge every act, even everything which is hidden, both good and bad.
ECCLESIASTES 12:13–14

Solomon ends his study of life by saying, "Honor God and obey His Laws." God is the one who one day will judge all you have done in life. So you should be careful to live in ways that honor Him. God gave you life so you would enjoy it, but you should enjoy it within the rules He has set for you. When you stand before Him, God will judge not only what you've done for yourself but especially what you've done for Him and others.

MOST BLESSED

(Song of Solomon 2:11–13)

MORNING PRAYER

Lord, Solomon wrote beautiful words about spring. Spring is a time of new beginnings as flowers bloom on trees, in bushes, and in gardens. The smell of flowers and rain fills the air. Birds sing as animals wake from hibernation. An explosion of color washes away the winter. Spring is here, celebrating the promise of eternal life—life in heaven, thanks to Jesus. Thank You, Lord! Amen.

EVENING DEVOTION

*If we have hope in Christ in this life only,
we are more sad than anyone else.*
1 CORINTHIANS 15:19

The heart of Christianity is Jesus' resurrection. When He died on the cross, our sins died with Him—we were forgiven. Jesus rose from the dead, just as we will one day. Through His resurrection, God promised us eternal life. Some people doubt the resurrection. Paul points out how sad this is. We have hope in Jesus not only in this life but in the next. Instead of the most miserable of all people, we are the most blessed and should be the most grateful.

FILTER

(1 Corinthians 15:55)

MORNING PRAYER

God, I wonder what heaven is like. My loved ones who are there will be waiting for me. I will finally be perfect and all You created me to be. I will join with my loved ones and the angels, praising You. I know there will be so much more for me in heaven than here on Earth. But until then, help me to make the most of my time here by serving You and others. Amen.

EVENING DEVOTION

O Lord, put a watch over my mouth. Keep watch over the door of my lips.
PSALM 141:3

Psalm 141:3 is a prayer we should pray every day—"O Lord, put a watch over my mouth. Keep watch over the door of my lips." How much less trouble we would get into if our thoughts and words were always filtered to please only God. What if everything we said built others up and honored God? What if our thoughts were always pure and lovely? Ask God to protect your words and even your thoughts.

CLEAN AS SNOW

(Isaiah 2:1–5)

MORNING PRAYER

Lord God, Isaiah's words create a picture. Your people from all over the world will gather at Your holy mountain to praise You. With that picture in my mind, I look forward to that day of peace when everyone on earth will know You, obey You, and follow You. But for today, God, let peace begin with me. Amen.

EVENING DEVOTION

"Wash yourselves. Make yourselves clean. . . . Stop doing sinful things. Learn to do good. Look for what is right and fair. Speak strong words to those who make it hard for people. . . . Come now, let us think about this together," says the Lord. "Even though your sins are bright red, they will be as white as snow. Even though they are dark red, they will be like wool."
ISAIAH 1:16–18

At the beginning of Isaiah 1, God speaks about all the evil His people have done. Then God tells us what we need to do to please Him—wash (clean up our hearts), put away evil, do good, and help those in need. Verse 18 reveals the result of doing these things—our bright red sins will be washed as clean as snow. This is how God deals with His people. He doesn't leave us alone in our sin.

FRUIT OF GRATEFULNESS
(2 Corinthians 1:1–11)

MORNING PRAYER

Dear God, I remember with gratefulness the times You've comforted me. Now, help me to comfort others. Open my eyes to those who are hurting. Teach me to listen and say the right words. Remind me not to speak about my own troubles but instead about how You have lifted me up with Your love and made things right again. Today, let me be an extension of You, sharing Your comfort and love with others. Amen.

EVENING DEVOTION

"And now, O people living in Jerusalem and men of Judah, judge between Me and My grape-field. What more was there to do for My grape-field that I have not done for it? When I expected it to give good grapes, why did it give wild grapes?"
Isaiah 5:3–4

God's parable—or story with a lesson—in Isaiah 5 provides a look into God's relationship with a sinful and ungrateful nation. The man in the story lovingly planted and tended to his vineyard only for it to rebel against Him, producing nothing but bad-tasting grapes. He asks, "What else could I have done for my vineyard?" It is an example of God pouring His blessings on us and us rebelling against Him. The best way to grow good fruit is by practicing gratefulness.

SEND ME
(Isaiah 6:6–7)

MORNING PRAYER

Lord God, I thank You for loving me enough to make me all I was created to be. When I experience Your correction, it might make me sad for a while, but not forever. Through Your gentle leading, I learn to be even more like You than I am today. Your correction cleans me of sin and gives me another chance to please You. Thank You, Lord, for guiding me through my life. Amen.

EVENING DEVOTION

Then I heard the voice of the Lord, saying, "Whom should I send? Who will go for Us?" Then I said, "Here am I. Send me!"
ISAIAH 6:8

Isaiah saw God in all His terrifying and majestic glory. When God asked who He should send, Isaiah immediately and firmly replied, "Here am I. Send me!" This is the only possible reaction of someone who has seen Almighty God. To know that God sits on His throne in power should inspire us to respond to His call to go and spread His gospel as readily and purposefully as Isaiah did.

KNOWN BY GOD
(Isaiah 9:1–7)

MORNING PRAYER

Jesus—Wonderful, Teacher, Powerful God, Father Who Lives Forever, Prince of Peace—Isaiah called You by these names when he announced to the world that You were coming. Did the people have any idea of how wonderful a gift You were preparing to send into the world, Father? Thank You, Jesus, for coming. Thank You for saving me from my sin and promising me the gift of eternal life. The older I get, the more I appreciate and value You. Amen.

EVENING DEVOTION

O Lord, what is man that You think of him, the son of man that You remember him? Man is like a breath. His days are like a passing shadow.
PSALM 144:3–4

Who are you that God should even notice you? Still, He cares for you more than you know. The depth of His love is beyond your understanding. Grasping just how much God knows and loves you would change your life. God's love is already changing you. Every time you seek Him through prayer and His Word, you grow in your relationship with Him. God's love will never change. He loves you now and forever.

BOLDNESS
(Psalm 145)

MORNING PRAYER

I praise You, Lord. The wonder of You fills my days. Forgive me when I allow bad talk to cross my lips. I want to speak of You and tell others how wonderful You are. I want to build people up, not tear them down. My words are never enough to measure Your greatness, but today and every day I will do my best to pass along the stories of Your goodness and love. Amen.

EVENING DEVOTION

We speak without fear because our trust is in Christ.
2 CORINTHIANS 3:12

How can we keep the good news to ourselves? Jesus came into the world, God as a human, and gave us the gift of forever life in heaven! We all should be bold when sharing that news. Maybe you feel uncomfortable sharing it. Maybe you feel you won't have the right words or people won't understand. Don't let those fears stop you. God will give you everything you need, even the boldness, to share the gospel.

GOD'S POWER
(Psalm 146)

MORNING PRAYER

I'm so blessed, God. Thanks to You, I have peace, joy, and hope. The God who created everything sees me. You know me and love me. You already have this day planned for me. You are so faithful all the time, and I ask that You will be faithful to those who need You the most. Use Your power today to help those who are worried or suffering, wherever they are. Amen.

EVENING DEVOTION

The Lord made heaven and earth, the sea and all that is in them. He is faithful forever. He helps those who have a bad power over them. He gives food to the hungry. And He sets those in prison free.
PSALM 146:6–7

God's power, as shown in His ability to create and sustain the entire universe, can't be compared to anything we know. But unlike so many humans who use power for personal gain, God uses His power to help those who are poor, hungry, lonely, and sad. God's power and wisdom can never be separated from His goodness, kindness, and love.

LOVE OF CHRIST
(2 Corinthians 5)

MORNING PRAYER

Heavenly Father, our world needs unity—people need to come together. I feel sad when I see the world divided with people taking sides. I pray today for togetherness. I want people to get along in spite of their differences. Even more, I want them, all of us, to be united with You through our belief in Jesus and our acceptance of His gift of forgiveness. Unite us, dear God, and let me help. Amen.

EVENING DEVOTION

For the love of Christ puts us into action. We are sure that Christ died for everyone. So, because of that, everyone has a part in His death. Christ died for everyone so that they would live for Him. They should not live to please themselves but for Christ Who died on a cross and was raised from the dead for them.
2 CORINTHIANS 5:14–15

Paul told the Corinthians that the love of Christ put him into action. What would it be like for Christ's love to lead you to act? Every action would be inspired by Jesus' love. Every word would share His love with others. Every prayer would be said as if you were standing before Jesus Himself. You would no longer live for yourself but for Him, Jesus, who gave up His life so you might truly live.

STRONG GATES

(2 Corinthians 6:3–10)

MORNING PRAYER

Lord, Paul was willing to be hated by others if it meant bringing people into Your kingdom. I think of others, like Martin Luther King Jr., who were willing to be hated for the sake of peace. If great people suffered to bring about good, then I should be willing to risk more of myself to tell others about Jesus. Even if it means some people won't like me, I'll choose to share the good news. Amen.

EVENING DEVOTION

For He has made your gates strong. He has made good come to your children within you.
PSALM 147:13

The author of today's psalm praised God for having made strong gates. In Bible times, because gates had to be able to open and close, they would be the weakest part of a walled city. It was extremely important for the gates to be strong. Do you know what your weakest places are when it comes to sin? Where in your life does sin creep in the easiest? Ask God to strengthen your "gates" and to help you be ready to protect those places.

GRACE AND FORGIVENESS

(Isaiah 24:14–17)

MORNING PRAYER

Lord God, everything on earth shouts praises to You, yet sometimes those praises are reduced to a whisper. The voice of sin tries to drown them out. But I hear You, Lord! I shout even louder over the voice of sin. I praise You because I am Your child. You always hear me and rescue me from evil. Thank You for showing me Your goodness and forgiveness every day. Amen.

EVENING DEVOTION

The sorrow that God uses makes people sorry for their sin and leads them to turn from sin so they can be saved from the punishment of sin. We should be happy for that kind of sorrow, but the sorrow of this world brings death.

2 CORINTHIANS 7:10

Paul spoke of the sadness we feel when we know we have displeased God. That kind of sadness is a good thing because it leads us to ask God to forgive us. Understanding that you've behaved badly and feeling sorry for it helps you not to behave that way again. When you feel sad about bad behavior, tell God. Then accept His forgiveness and move on without guilt. Ask Him to help you do better next time.

HE IS WORTHY
(Psalm 150)

MORNING PRAYER

Dear God, what a beautiful morning for me to praise You. What a great day for all the earth to praise You. Let the praises of creation echo all the way to heaven. Let everything on earth, from the rippling waterfalls to trees rustling in the wind, bring glory to Your name. Let everything that has breath—from the bee that buzzes to the whale that sings to the newborn baby who cries—praise You. God, You are so worthy of praise. Amen.

EVENING DEVOTION

*Let everything that has breath praise
the Lord. Praise the Lord!*
PSALM 150:6

Psalm 150 portrays a powerful picture of what God's creation will be like one day. Everything that has breath will praise the Lord. In the meantime, our praise of Him should fill our lives and spill over into the lives of others. God is worthy of praise simply because of who He is—the almighty God. But He is also worthy because of the wonderful things He does. Praise Him now and continue to praise Him until the whole earth and the entire universe join in.

NEVER GIVE UP
(2 Corinthians 9:6–8)

MORNING PRAYER

Dear God, Thank You for the joy of giving. Show me where and to whom and to what to give. Let me give endlessly of non-money gifts like prayer and my time. And if I have some money to give, let me give it wisely. I'm grateful You always make sure I have everything I need for every good work and also for generous giving. Amen.

EVENING DEVOTION

So the Lord wants to show you kindness. He waits on high to have loving-pity on you. For the Lord is a God of what is right and fair. And good will come to all those who hope in Him.
ISAIAH 30:18

Just as loving parents wait for their children to behave, so will God wait patiently for you to obey Him. He will not get fed up with you. You won't be able to try His patience beyond what He can handle. He wants you to follow Him and keep His commandments. He will never give up on those who are His.

YOUR THOUGHTS
(2 Corinthians 10:5)

MORNING PRAYER

Father, I struggle with my thoughts, especially when someone or something tries to lead me into sin. I give my thoughts to You. Give me wisdom to bring all my thoughts in line with Yours. Plant the scripture verses I've memorized firmly in my mind so I can recall them whenever I feel confused. Hide Your Word in my heart and lead me into right thinking. Amen.

EVENING DEVOTION

We do not use those things to fight with that the world uses. We use the things God gives to fight with and they have power. Those things God gives to fight with destroy the strong-places of the devil. We break down every thought and proud thing that puts itself up against the wisdom of God. We take hold of every thought and make it obey Christ.
2 CORINTHIANS 10:4–5

Too often we struggle with thoughts that lead us toward sin. We should be grateful that God gives us everything we need to fight against them. His power works through us. Ask God to help you bring every thought in line with the way Jesus thinks. Imagine how different and better your life might become. God, in His great power, will help you overcome every wrong thought, even those you think in secret.

POWER OF GOD
(Isaiah 35)

MORNING PRAYER

Lord God, I want to get in shape, both physically and mentally. Help me to become strong, the best I can be. I pray this morning for all who are weak and struggling. Please use Your power to heal minds and bodies. I know You will perform wonders. I might not see all the ways You answer this prayer here on earth, but I trust in Your power and Your answer of. . .yes! Amen.

EVENING DEVOTION

*If I must talk about myself, I will do it about
the things that show how weak I am.*
2 CORINTHIANS 11:30

Paul didn't care much about personal appearance. In fact, if he were to brag, he would brag about the very things most of us would want to keep hidden. He talked about the embarrassing times he had to be rescued when he wandered into trouble. But instead of focusing on what he did, Paul told how God's power rescued him. Become a man like Paul, ready to tell the stories that make you "look bad" but show the goodness and power of God.

MAKER OF HEAVEN AND EARTH

(2 Corinthians 12:9–10)

MORNING PRAYER

Dear God, I'm feeling weak and not well prepared for today. I'm not sure I can accomplish what I have waiting for me to do. I need You to give me Your strength. I'll be happy with whatever I accomplish. However it turns out, I'll tell others about my weakness and the good that came from it because of You. Open my eyes to Your goodness, God. Lead me into this day. Amen.

EVENING DEVOTION

*Whom have you put to shame and spoken against?
Against whom have you raised your voice and lifted up
your eyes in pride? Against the Holy One of Israel!*
ISAIAH 37:23

Those who say bad things about others are really saying bad things about God Himself. Maybe people have made fun of you for being a Christian. God is standing right beside you. It's as if they are making fun of Him too. It is God those people are against. It might be easy for some to talk badly about other human beings, but talking against the Maker of heaven and earth is never a good idea.

GENTLE SHEPHERD

(Isaiah 40:28–29)

MORNING PRAYER

Heavenly Father, You don't say, "See you later," or hang a sign saying Out to Lunch. You don't come and go. You are here for me 24/7, 365 days a year. The way You care for me doesn't change. I never need to feel overlooked or forgotten. You know all there is to know about everything. You are an awesome God, sharing all Your energy, power, and strength with me every day. Amen.

EVENING DEVOTION

See, the Lord God will come with power, and His arm will rule for Him. See, He is bringing the reward He will give to everyone for what he has done. He will feed His flock like a shepherd. He will gather the lambs in His arms and carry them close to His heart. He will be gentle in leading those that are with young.

ISAIAH 40:10–11

Notice the powerful contrast in Isaiah 40:10–11. Verse 10 pictures God as a strong warrior-king coming to rule the earth with power and strength. Verse 11 changes the image to that of a caring shepherd who carries lambs in His arms and gently leads His sheep. We serve a God who is so powerful that He conquered death and evil and yet is so good and loving that He gently leads and cares for us. In Him, we find true protection and rest.

CHOSEN
(Isaiah 41)

MORNING PRAYER

Dear God, thank You for choosing me. Thank You for loving me. When people hear my name, I want them to think well of me—and most importantly, to be drawn to You too. After all, I want to live up to my family's reputation—I am a chosen son of God. Today and every day, I choose to live right so I can bring honor to Your name and mine. Amen.

EVENING DEVOTION

"I have taken you from the ends of the earth. I have called you from its farthest parts, and said to you, 'You are My servant. I have chosen you and have not turned away from you.' Do not fear, for I am with you. Do not be afraid, for I am your God. I will give you strength, and for sure I will help you. Yes, I will hold you up with My right hand. . . . For I am the Lord your God Who holds your right hand, and Who says to you, 'Do not be afraid. I will help you.'"
ISAIAH 41:9–10, 13

God has chosen you. He set you aside as one of His children before the world was formed. You have nothing to fear when you understand that your whole life was planned far in advance by a loving Father. And in those times when you do feel afraid, He holds you up to make you strong. Listen as He says to you, "Do not be afraid. I will help you."

ISAIAH 43:1–44:20
GALATIANS 2
PROVERBS 3:1–12

FULLY LOVED
(Isaiah 43:16–21)

MORNING PRAYER

Heavenly Father, sometimes I struggle to let go of my mistakes. Please help me to stop thinking about all the ways I've messed up. Open my eyes to the new road You are making for me. Help me leave my mistakes far behind as I move forward with You. Your ways are good and pleasant. The past is the past. You, God, are my future. Amen.

EVENING DEVOTION

"You are of great worth in My eyes. You are honored and I love you. I will give other men in your place. I will trade other people for your life."
ISAIAH 43:4

Do you truly believe that you are precious to God? Do you believe He loves you as fully as He says? Do you believe He would go to the ends of the earth to bring you back? Because we're so familiar with imperfect, worldly love, we often struggle to believe we could be loved so perfectly and fully by God. Believe that your heavenly Father, who considers you a beloved son, will prove His love for you as He works daily to bring you closer to Him.

WISE BEHAVIOR
(Isaiah 45:22–24)

MORNING PRAYER

Dear God, You say that every knee will bow before You. I'm blessed today because of people around me who loved You, honored You, and knelt before You in prayer. I thank You that they are my family and friends. If I have children and they have children and my grandchildren have children, I pray that all of them will be faithful and honor You. Amen.

EVENING DEVOTION

The Lord built the earth by wisdom. He built the heavens by understanding. By what He knows, the seas were broken up and water falls from the sky.
PROVERBS 3:19–20

The book of Proverbs has plenty to say about wisdom— why we should value it, how we should search for it, and what wise behavior looks like. Why is wisdom so important? Because it is one of the characteristics of God. With wisdom, He created the earth and the universe. Gaining wisdom makes us more like God. To be more like Him is truly of more value than anything else we treasure.

GLORY OF GOD
(Isaiah 48:10–11)

MORNING PRAYER

Father, You won't let anything take Your rightful place as Lord of my life. You love me, test me, and discipline me. I praise You because everything You do for me comes from Your heart of love. You chose me to be Yours and to serve You here on earth. I will do my best to serve You well and give You all the glory. Amen.

EVENING DEVOTION

The Lord Who bought you and saves you, the Holy One of Israel, says, "I am the Lord your God, Who teaches you to do well, Who leads you in the way you should go."
ISAIAH 48:17

Do you have idols in your life—things you love more than God? Sports? Video games? Your phone? Girls? All of these can become idols if we love them more than God. Most of the time we aren't even aware of our idols. Ask God to open your eyes to those things you hold as more important than Him. Ask for His forgiveness. Then do your best to always put God first.

EVERLASTING GOD
(Isaiah 49:18)

MORNING PRAYER

Lord God, You say I should lift up my eyes and see all those who are gathered together in Your kingdom. Here on earth, we gather together in church and elsewhere to worship and praise You. I think it must be a beautiful sight to You, Lord, when Your people gather together. We will worship You now and forever, our everlasting God. Amen.

EVENING DEVOTION

"I, even I, am He Who comforts you. Who are you that you are afraid of a man who dies? Why are you afraid of the sons of men who are made like grass, that you have forgotten the Lord Who made you? He spread out the heavens and put the earth in its place. Why do you live in fear all day long because of the anger of the one who makes it hard for you?"
ISAIAH 51:12–13

Why are we afraid of other people's opinions about us and the power they have over us? We get so caught up in what other people think. The one whose opinion matters most is God. He has enormous power that would make even the strongest of humans afraid. The opinions others have about us will fade away, but what God thinks is everlasting. Whose opinion matters to you the most?

GUARD YOUR HEART

(Galatians 4:27)

MORNING PRAYER

Dear Jesus, today's Bible verse is a reminder that You came first for the Jewish people. Then You offered Your gift of salvation to those who weren't Jews. You welcomed the whole world into Your family. How sad it would be if You hadn't come for all of us—but You would never leave us alone and forgotten. Thank You for making us Your children. I'm glad Your family gets bigger every day. Amen.

EVENING DEVOTION

*Keep your heart pure for out of it are
the important things of life.*
PROVERBS 4:23

Honor God by guarding your heart. Keep it pure. Don't fill it with worthless wants and empty entertainment. Be more concerned about your own heart than anyone else's. Worry about your sins more than the sins of your friends and family. Remember that Jesus lives in your heart. Do your best to be like Him; then others will see Him in you.

SALVATION
(Isaiah 56:6–8)

MORNING PRAYER

Father God, I'm so grateful that Jesus saved us from sin. His gift is available to everyone, if only they'll take it. Keep working on those who don't want His gift! Bring people into their lives who know You and are ready to share about Jesus with them. Reach people all over the world. Lead them to accept the gifts of Your forgiveness and forever life in heaven. Amen.

EVENING DEVOTION

Christ made us free. Stay that way. Do not get chained all over again in the Law and its kind of religious worship.

GALATIANS 5:1

In Old Testament days, God's people had many rules to follow—and they couldn't obey them all. Jesus came to change that. God sent Jesus so we would be forgiven for every rule we break. Thanks to Jesus, you don't have to earn your way to forgiveness or eternal life in heaven. Accepting Him as your Savior is enough. It is because we are grateful that we choose to honor and serve Him.

ISAIAH 58–59
GALATIANS 6
PROVERBS 5:15–23

WHERE IS YOUR HEART?

(Galatians 6:7–10)

MORNING PRAYER

Dear God, help me not to get tired of doing good. Sometimes I don't get any recognition for the ways I try to help others, but that shouldn't matter. I want to remember that every bit of work I do for others is really for You. My heart needs to be in the right place, remembering how often You go without thanks for the good things You do. Forgive me, God, for the times I've forgotten to thank You. Amen.

EVENING DEVOTION

"Is it not a time to share your food with the hungry, and bring the poor man into your house who has no home of his own? Is it not a time to give clothes to the person you see who has no clothes, and a time not to hide yourself from your own family? Then your light will break out like the early morning, and you will soon be healed. Your right and good works will go before you. And the shining-greatness of the Lord will keep watch behind you. Then you will call, and the Lord will answer. You will cry, and He will say, 'Here I am.'"
ISAIAH 58:7–9

God promises to bless us when we help others. While reading the Bible, you've likely discovered many stories about God helping people—that's what He does! His help is impossible to miss. God's heart is forever filled with caring for those in need. Is your heart like His? Are you always ready and willing to help?

PURE LOVE
(Isaiah 61)

MORNING PRAYER

Dear God, it seems I'm closest to You on my worst days. That's when I lean into Your love and rest in Your comfort. It might sound strange, but I'm thankful for those bad days when I run to You. I want to shout for joy because You are always with me. You know how to fix my problems and make me feel better. God, I am so grateful for Your endless pure love. Amen.

EVENING DEVOTION

Even before the world was made, God chose us for Himself because of His love. He planned that we should be holy and without blame as He sees us. God already planned to have us as His own children. This was done by Jesus Christ. In His plan God wanted this done.
EPHESIANS 1:4–5

God chose you as His child even before He made the earth. He planned long ago that you would be His, made holy and blameless through Jesus and His love. He did all this simply because it pleased Him to do so. There is no other reason. A love so full and pure is impossible to understand, but it's something for us to be grateful for, every single day.

ISAIAH 63:1–65:16
EPHESIANS 2
PROVERBS 6:6–19

GOD'S DESIRE
(Ephesians 2)

MORNING PRAYER

Jesus, when I mess up, I do my best to catch myself and ask for Your forgiveness. And always, You forgive me. You free me from past mistakes and let me start over again. You protect me and lead me in Your ways. I know You desire for me to lead a sinless life. Thank You, Jesus, that when sin catches me off guard and I fall into its trap, You pick me up and forgive me again. Amen.

EVENING DEVOTION

He did this to show us through all the time to come the great riches of His loving-favor. He has shown us His kindness through Christ Jesus.
EPHESIANS 2:7

Ephesians 2 lists some things God has done for you: He created you, loved you, saved you, and promised you eternal life in heaven. Why would He do all this for you? Does He want something in return? The answer comes in verse 7— He did these things so, through Jesus, He might show you goodness and kindness. He wants to shower you with love and forgiveness. How undeserving we are to belong to a God who is so selflessly good to us.

UNDERSTANDING GOD'S LOVE
(Ephesians 4:4)

MORNING PRAYER

Lord God, You give me forever hope—hope that, one day, I will see Jesus in heaven and be with all the other Christians who love and honor Him. In the meantime, I want to share that hope with the world. I want to tell everyone of Your great love. Help me to stand strong, united with other Christians on earth, to share the hope of eternal life with You. Amen.

EVENING DEVOTION

I pray that you will know the love of Christ. His love goes beyond anything we can understand. I pray that you will be filled with God Himself.
EPHESIANS 3:19

Paul prayed that the Ephesians would know the amazing love of Jesus—a love that is beyond anyone's understanding. He wanted them to know that Jesus' love for us is so huge that our human minds cannot grasp it. But to know even the smallest bit of His love is life-changing. Ask God to begin to help you understand the power of Jesus' love.

TAKE COURAGE
(Ephesians 4:22–27)

MORNING PRAYER

Lord Jesus, make my spirit new today. Clean it up. Fill me with a new attitude so I will be more like You in my actions and words. Help me get rid of any hurt and anger. Replace them with caring and forgiveness. Guide me to build others up and not tear them down. Give me a loving spirit. I trust in Your help, Lord. I'm ready for today. Let's go! Amen.

EVENING DEVOTION

"Before I started to put you together in your mother, I knew you. Before you were born, I set you apart as holy. I chose you to speak to the nations for Me."
JEREMIAH 1:5

God had planned Jeremiah's whole life before he was born. God already knew Jeremiah better than anyone would ever know him. God was the Lord of Jeremiah's life, just as He is the Lord of your life if you've accepted Jesus as your Savior. On difficult days, have courage. God knows what's going on with you. He knew about it before it happened; you don't have to fill Him in, but He does want to hear from you. He is perfect to go to with your worries and prayers.

SIN

(Jeremiah 4:3–4)

MORNING PRAYER

Father God, You say I should set myself apart to You. I think that means I should reject all things that displease You and instead follow Your will. God, You give me freedom to decide. Either I can do what I know is wrong, or I can make the best decision and walk away from sin and set myself apart from it. Remind me always to choose well. Amen.

EVENING DEVOTION

*Have nothing to do with the bad things done in
darkness. Instead, show that these things are wrong.*
EPHESIANS 5:11

Don't allow yourself to slip into sin, especially things done in secret. Instead, tell God about those things you want to do that might displease Him. You also might consider talking with older, trusted Christians who can help you decide between right and wrong. Talking about your struggles can take a load off your mind and lead you nearer to God's will.

JEREMIAH 4:23–5:31
EPHESIANS 6
PROVERBS 7:6–27

SPREAD GOD'S LIGHT
(Ephesians 6:1–3)

MORNING PRAYER

God, forgive me for not always following your command to honor my parents. I know they love me and are doing their best to raise me. You set me in this family; this is where You want me. That alone is reason to treat my parents and other family members with respect. Please fill my home with peace and love. And when I disobey my parents, remind me to apologize and ask for forgiveness. Amen.

EVENING DEVOTION

Our fight is not with people. It is against the leaders and the powers and the spirits of darkness in this world. It is against the demon world that works in the heavens.
EPHESIANS 6:12

An unseen war is happening in the world. It is a war between good and evil. Paul spoke about evil as darkness. We can conquer that darkness by sharing God's love—His light—all over the world. Sharing God's Word with others and talking about Him can help both us and those around us to stand up to evil. Prayer helps too. Someday Jesus will come and wipe all evil from the earth, but in the meantime, we are His soldiers. Our mission is to spread His light everywhere we go.

FULLY TRUST
(Philippians 1:4–11)

MORNING PRAYER

Heavenly Father, Paul said You began a good work in me. He felt sure You would lead me through the plans You have for my life, and You wouldn't be done with me until I see You in heaven one day. I feel safe knowing You are always with me. I know I can trust You. Work Your plan for me, God. I am willing to go wherever You lead. Amen.

EVENING DEVOTION

I am sure that God Who began the good work in you will keep on working in you until the day Jesus Christ comes again.
PHILIPPIANS 1:6

God is a promise keeper. He has proven His faithfulness throughout history. You can trust Him to fulfill His promise that He will make perfect the good work He has started in you. This means that no sin, guilt, or lack of motivation can keep Him from working in your life. Your own feelings of insecurity can't get in the way because God will help you find a way around them. God will make perfect His work that He started in you. You can count on it.

CAUSE OF CHRIST
(Jeremiah 8:20–22)

MORNING PRAYER

Lord, sometimes I foolishly go my own way looking for help when it would be best just to go to You. I look everywhere else for answers when You have all the wisdom. Forgive me. Open my ears to Your voice. Lead me to the Bible. Remind me to follow Your commands. Show me what to do to keep every decision and every step in line with Your will. Amen.

EVENING DEVOTION

Be glad you can do the things you should be doing. Do all things without arguing and talking about how you wish you did not have to do them. In that way, you can prove yourselves to be without blame. You are God's children and no one can talk against you, even in a sin-loving and sin-sick world. You are to shine as lights among the sinful people of this world.
PHILIPPIANS 2:14–15

Each day you have the opportunity to shine God's light on the world. Doing everything without grumbling or complaining makes those watching realize there is something different about you. Choosing instead to go along with the world's grumblings and arguments would do nothing to teach others about Jesus. Look for ways to bring the news of Jesus everywhere you go. Let the world know through the way you live that you are a son of God.

FIND YOUR WORTH
(Jeremiah 9:23–24)

MORNING PRAYER

Heavenly Father, if I think I'm smart, wise, strong, or popular—even if it's true—those attributes don't come from me. They come from You as Your good gifts. Sometimes I struggle with how to share my good news without feeling like I'm bragging. Guide me to form my news with You at the center. Keep me focused on what I've learned from You when I speak of the good things You've done through me. Amen.

EVENING DEVOTION

The Lord says, "Let not a wise man speak with pride about his wisdom. Let not the strong man speak with pride about his strength. And let not a rich man speak with pride about his riches. But let him who speaks with pride speak about this, that he understands and knows Me, that I am the Lord who shows loving-kindness and does what is fair and right and good on earth. For I find joy in these things," says the Lord.
JEREMIAH 9:23–24

What makes you think you are valuable? Are you strong? Good at sports? Good-looking? Popular? Smart? All these things can be gifts from God, but the only thing in which you should find your worth is knowing the Lord. Belonging to God is a privilege. More than anything else, work to be well known because of how deeply you know your Savior.

STUMBLING
(Proverbs 9:1–6)

MORNING PRAYER

Father, Your Word is like a banquet spread before me. There are so many excellent scripture verses to sample. Each increases my wisdom and presents new truths about You. I can never get enough. I could feast on Your Word forever. Every time I open my Bible to read, I discover something new. You open my mind to fresh ideas and help me see the world not through my eyes but through Yours. Amen.

EVENING DEVOTION

I want to be as one with Him. I could not be right with God by what the Law said I must do. I was made right with God by faith in Christ.

PHILIPPIANS 3:9

The famous followers of Christ in the Bible were not perfect people. Just like Christians today, they became aware of their imperfections, and because of them, they learned to rely more on Jesus. When an obstacle made them stumble, they sometimes fell into sin, but they knew who would pick them up. Christ's followers are always rescued by His goodness.

NO WORRIES
(Philippians 4:7)

MORNING PRAYER

Dear Jesus, Prince of Peace, I ask You to give me a peaceful day. Guard my heart and mind with Your peace. Help me to be content and calm when things get busy or if I face a problem. Lead me into this new day with joy. I should have no worries because You will be with me all day long. Amen.

EVENING DEVOTION

Do not worry. Learn to pray about everything. Give thanks to God as you ask Him for what you need.
PHILIPPIANS 4:6

The apostle Paul felt certain worry was of no benefit. He was sure nothing was too big or difficult for God to handle. When we're anxious, we're basically questioning whether God is able to do the right thing. We have no reason to be anxious. God is always in control. Bring your worries to Him and leave them there. Then thank God for taking them and doing what's best.

JEREMIAH 16–17
COLOSSIANS 1:1–23
PROVERBS 10:1–5

PLEASE THE LORD
(Jeremiah 17:7–10)

MORNING PRAYER

Lord God, You said good comes to people who hope in You. They are like trees planted near water, never thirsty even on the hottest days. I know if I trust in You I will be blessed. Your words remind me to keep watch over my heart so it won't be fooled by evil. Lord, look into my heart. Change what needs changing so my behavior will be worthy of Your blessing. Amen.

EVENING DEVOTION

This is why I have never stopped praying for you since I heard about you. I ask God that you may know what He wants you to do. I ask God to fill you with the wisdom and understanding the Holy Spirit gives. Then your lives will please the Lord. You will do every kind of good work, and you will know more about God.
COLOSSIANS 1:9–10

Paul never stopped praying for the Colossians, asking God that they would be filled with knowledge and wisdom and that they would "please the Lord" in good works. Is there anything you care about enough to never stop praying for it? Think about praying for yourself in the same way Paul did for the Colossians—ask God to fill you with knowledge and wisdom so everything you do will please Him.

TRUE VICTORY
(Proverbs 10:12)

MORNING PRAYER

Dear God, if hate starts fights, then it starts in my mind and heart. *Hate* is a strong word. I hope any negative feelings I have toward others don't boil into hatred. You expect better from me. You want me to cover my negative feelings with love instead of responding with hate. You are the perfect example. Make me like You. Amen.

EVENING DEVOTION

*We had broken the Law many ways. Those sins were
held against us by the Law. That Law had writings
which said we were sinners. But now He has destroyed
that writing by nailing it to the cross. God took
away the power of the leaders of this world and the
powers of darkness. He showed them to the world.
The battle was won over them through Christ.*
COLOSSIANS 2:14–15

Satan must have thought he'd achieved a victory, overcoming God's power, when he saw Jesus on the cross. Little did Satan know that moment represented his greatest loss. Jesus' death for our sin took away all the power Satan had over us. Jesus destroyed it when He died on the cross, and through Him, we are forgiven, forever, here on earth and in heaven. And there's nothing Satan can do to change that.

IT IS WELL

(Jeremiah 20:14–18)

MORNING PRAYER

Heavenly Father, Jeremiah was a great man, and yet he felt worthless. I feel like that sometimes. I feel down when things aren't going my way. I think I must be doing something wrong. I realize You can't use me when I feel worthless, so please lift me out of my depression. Give me a positive attitude. Lighten my heart and mind so I can get back to working for You. Amen.

EVENING DEVOTION

"He spoke strong words in the cause of the poor and those in need, and so all went well. Is not that what it means to know Me?" says the Lord.

JEREMIAH 22:16

What is it to know God? God said King Josiah knew Him because he spoke up for the poor and needy. We could probably think of far more glamorous ways to know God. And yet this is what God says it means to know Him. Could His heart for those in need be any clearer? People can be poor in many areas, not just in terms of money—in need of things like comfort, learning, laughter, confidence. . . . What can you do to help today?

LET PEACE RULE

(Colossians 3:12–13)

MORNING PRAYER

Lord God, I care about how I look, but I need to remember that clothing myself in goodness is more important than any current fashion. I want to wear compassion, kindness, gentleness, patience, and peace. I don't want people to look at me and think, *He's all that.* I want them to see me and think, *He belongs to God.* Add to my wardrobe, Father. Dress me like a citizen of Your kingdom. Amen.

EVENING DEVOTION

Let the peace of Christ have power over your hearts. You were chosen as a part of His body. Always be thankful.
COLOSSIANS 3:15

Paul didn't say to *make* the peace of Christ rule in your heart or even to ask for it. You only need to *let* peace rule. God's peace already exists in your heart. So if you're worried and anxious trying to figure out your life, let His peace rule your every thought and action instead. Don't allow any room for doubt or fear to separate you from His peace.

YOUR HEART IS HIS
(Jeremiah 24:4–7)

MORNING PRAYER

God, did men like Daniel, Ezekiel, and Mordecai realize they'd been sent away from Israel for their good? You protected them. You sent them to a place where they would prosper. You wanted to build them up, not tear them down, and give them hearts to know You. Maybe that's why You have redirected me from my plans. I'm sure You have something better waiting for me. Lead me in the way I should go. Amen.

EVENING DEVOTION

"And I will give them a heart to know Me, for I am the Lord. They will be My people and I will be their God, for they will return to Me with their whole heart."
JEREMIAH 24:7

God gives you a heart to know Him. On your own you would be helpless in seeking Him. But God wants you to know Him, and He doesn't hide from you. He has given you all you need to know Him. The Lord directs the hearts of everyone on earth; He can turn hearts whichever way He chooses. If your heart is His, it always will be.

SECRET KEEPER
(1 Thessalonians 1:2–3)

JEREMIAH 26–27
1 THESSALONIANS 1:1–2:8
PROVERBS 11:12–21

MORNING PRAYER

Father, what do people think of me? I hope they see me as a reflection of You. Maybe the things I do, the ways I behave, can lead them nearer to You. Maybe when they see my strong faith in You, they will want to believe in You and trust You too. Help me to set a good example for others but also to be humble, remembering that my goodness comes from You. Amen.

EVENING DEVOTION

*He who is always telling stories makes secrets known,
but he who can be trusted keeps a thing hidden.*
PROVERBS 11:13

Many arguments and ruined relationships are caused by gossip—talking about others behind their backs. Gossip often includes made-up stories or broken trust. Sadly, gossip tears people down. If you feel tempted to pass along gossip or to betray something told to you in secret, stop. Think about how it might affect others. Think about God and what He wants you to do.

JEREMIAH 28–29
1 THESSALONIANS 2:9–3:13
PROVERBS 11:22–26

LOVE ONE ANOTHER

(Jeremiah 29:11–13)

MORNING PRAYER

Lord, seeking You is like being in a maze and finding little hints of You along the way. Each hint leads me nearer to You. I won't get out of this maze called life until I meet You in heaven, but until then, I'm enjoying the walk. With each step I take, I understand more about You. One day I will come out into the light of Your love and find You seated on Your throne. Amen.

EVENING DEVOTION

May the Lord make you grow in love for each other and for everyone. We have this kind of love for you. May our God and Father make your hearts strong and without blame. May your hearts be without sin in God's sight when our Lord Jesus comes again with all those who belong to Him.

1 THESSALONIANS 3:12–13

Paul prayed that the Thessalonians' love would increase for each other and for all people. Love is a key message of the gospel. God's love is not the kind of love that allows people to do whatever they want as long as it makes them happy. Instead, it's the kind of love that encourages others to live their lives pleasing God. What does "love" mean to you? How does your definition compare with God's kind of love?

STILL, HE LOVES
(Proverbs 11:30)

MORNING PRAYER

Heavenly Father, I can be foolish and self-serving sometimes. Each day, You shower me with "fruit"—Your blessings. But I sometimes forget that they aren't mine alone. Your blessings are meant to be shared. Open my eyes to ways I can share my blessings with others. Each blessing is like a seed I can sow to plant more trees that will bear more fruit. Blessings shared create more blessings, and all of them come from You. Amen.

EVENING DEVOTION

The Lord came to us from far away, saying, "I have loved you with a love that lasts forever. So I have helped you come to Me with loving-kindness."

JEREMIAH 31:3

Even when God disciplines His children, He still loves them. In fact, it's because He loves them that He disciplines them. No matter what trouble God brings you through, His love is everlasting. It will never be taken from you or fail you. With loving-kindness, God will draw you near. As you grow older, you will see more and more evidence of His love threading all the way through your life.

IN THE HURT

(Jeremiah 31:31–36)

MORNING PRAYER

Almighty God, I'm so grateful that You promised us Jesus and then sent Him here to earth. You remade us by forgiving our sins. You set Your commands in our hearts, but knowing how imperfect we are at keeping them, You made a way to heaven for us through Jesus' death on the cross. You live in my heart now, and all I want to do is please You. God, You are the Lord of All. Amen.

EVENING DEVOTION

*The One Who called you is faithful
and will do what He promised.*

1 THESSALONIANS 5:24

We all know the feeling of being let down, watching promises get broken, seeing dreams fade away. In life we can expect to be disappointed and hurt. That's why it's important to remember God will never fail us. He is perfectly faithful. What He has promised to do He will do, never changing His mind. It's in our everyday troubles that we begin to more fully appreciate how faithful He is.

GOD'S TIME AND ENERGY
(Jeremiah 33:6–9)

MORNING PRAYER

Lord God, You answered Jeremiah's prayers with powerful promises. You planned to do wonderful, amazing things, but with one single purpose—to glorify You. As you brought about good in answer to Jeremiah's prayers, You received praise and honor. People from all over the world wanted to know You. That was true in Jeremiah's time just as it is today. Lord, please provide what I ask for in prayer, yet not for my sake, but for Your glory. Amen.

EVENING DEVOTION

"Call to Me, and I will answer you. And I will show you great and wonderful things which you do not know."
JEREMIAH 33:3

The God of the universe promises that if you call on Him, He will answer you. He doesn't just promise to give a quick answer and then move on. Not at all. He spends time with you, guides and teaches you, and shows you great and mighty things. Think about how small and seemingly insignificant you are in the universe. Yet God chooses to invest an infinite amount of His energy and time in you.

DOING GOOD

(2 Thessalonians 3:16)

MORNING PRAYER

Prince of Peace, I pray You will spread Your peace at all times and in every way. I want a perfect personal peace, but I pray also for peace for others. You are with all Your people, and I always want to be at peace with my friends, family, and even those I don't know. Lord, today I will make peace my goal. Amen.

EVENING DEVOTION

But you, Christian brothers, do not get tired of doing good.
2 THESSALONIANS 3:13

"Do not get tired of doing good." Doing good should not just be something you do sometimes. It should be a lifestyle, something that defines who you are. The power of a kind word, a listening ear, or time taken out of your day for someone else is always welcome. Reach out to others. See if you can help meet their needs. Serve them as an example of what Jesus did when He lived on the earth.

GOOD OR BAD

(Proverbs 13:2–3)

MORNING PRAYER

Lord, Solomon made wise comparisons. What is bad? What is good? I know I can turn to his proverbs for advice. Today's Bible passage reminds me to watch what I say. My words can bring about good, or they can cause trouble. Teach me to be wise like Solomon, and today help me to watch my words. Amen.

EVENING DEVOTION

*He who watches over his mouth keeps his life.
He who opens his lips wide will be destroyed.*

PROVERBS 13:3

It's no mistake that the Bible emphasizes the dangers of what comes out of our mouths. Think about times when you let words slip that you weren't proud of. Would you have fewer regrets if you had kept your mouth shut, as Solomon advises in Proverbs? Good words lift people up. They make life better. But bad speech causes nothing but trouble.

JEREMIAH 38:14–40:6
1 TIMOTHY 1:18–3:13
PROVERBS 13:5–13

RICHES
(Proverbs 13:10)

MORNING PRAYER

Father God, too often I want to be right. Forgive me. Help me to understand that not everyone thinks the way I do. I want to listen with respect to other ideas and consider them. Lead me away from my pride and guide me toward wisdom and truth. Teach me to recognize the wisdom that comes from You and not to rely only on my own thoughts or those of others. Amen.

EVENING DEVOTION

There is one who pretends to be rich, but has nothing.
Another pretends to be poor, but has many riches.
PROVERBS 13:7

What do you value? What would make you rich? Does "rich" mean you have a lot of money and stuff, or does wealth come from what's in your heart? Your greatest treasure is your relationship with God. Every good thing you do on earth adds to your treasure chest in heaven. Work at becoming rich by being God's servant on earth and leading others to His kingdom.

SPIRITUAL FITNESS
(1 Timothy 4:6–10)

MORNING PRAYER

Lord Jesus, I think fitness is important, but Paul's words today make me stop and think. They tell me that having a fitness plan is good, but having a plan for godly living is better. Keep me from getting sidetracked. Help me first to strive toward spiritual fitness and then to keep my body healthy and strong. Amen.

EVENING DEVOTION

*Growing strong in body is all right but growing in
God-like living is more important. It will not only
help you in this life now but in the next life also.*
1 TIMOTHY 4:8

Physical exercise is healthy and good, but it's only worth something in this lifetime. Spiritual exercise—working to live a godly life—is worthy not only in this lifetime but also in eternal life in heaven. Put the same effort into spiritual fitness as an Olympian would put into physical fitness. Set aside time for "training." Think about God's Word throughout the day. As you fall asleep tonight, recite Bible verses you've memorized.

DAY 302

JEREMIAH 43–44
1 TIMOTHY 4:11–5:16
PROVERBS 13:22–25

DESIRE FOR GOD
(Proverbs 13:22)

MORNING PRAYER

Father, as I learn about You, I realize I'm storing up treasures. Each scripture verse I memorize, every time I read the Bible and think about its words, I become richer in my spirit. My heart becomes fuller with You. If I become a dad someday, I want to pass what I've learned about You to my children. I want their lives to be marked by faith and love and holy living. Amen.

EVENING DEVOTION

*But the one who lives only for the joy she can receive
from this world is the same as dead even if she is alive.*
1 TIMOTHY 5:6

Do you love going out and having a good time with your friends? Every guy does. But be careful that your good times don't lead you away from the Lord. When you give in to sin, it creeps into your heart and kills a little of your godly spirit. If you aren't careful, sin can take over God's place in your heart. It's great to have fun. Be joyful! Just be sure the kind of fun you have is pleasing to God.

CONTENTMENT
(Jeremiah 45:5)

JEREMIAH 45–47
1 TIMOTHY 5:17–6:21
PROVERBS 14:1–6

MORNING PRAYER

Heavenly Father, I want everything in my life to be comfortable, successful, easy, good, and right. How selfish of me to want everything for myself when I see people around me who are in need. Teach me to be satisfied with the small things. You have always brought me through hard times. Help me to be someone who does that for others—someone who helps to meet the needs of others, to bless them, and to spur them on in their relationship with God. Amen.

EVENING DEVOTION

A God-like life gives us much when we are happy for what we have. We came into this world with nothing. For sure, when we die, we will take nothing with us. If we have food and clothing, let us be happy.
1 TIMOTHY 6:6–8

Paul's words about contentment are worth thinking about. Why would we want more than we have when we understand that we brought nothing into this world and can take nothing out of it? The simple things we need to live are all we really need. The rest of what we have is a blessing and a gift from God. Be grateful for what God has given you.

JEREMIAH 48:1–49:6
2 TIMOTHY 1
PROVERBS 14:7–22

EVERLASTING LIFE
(2 Timothy 1:3–8)

MORNING PRAYER

Lord Jesus, I thank You for those who pray for me night and day. I feel their prayers in my heart. They want what's best for me, and they ask for You to lead me into a life that's pleasing to You. Thank You, Jesus, for Your Holy Spirit who whispers prayers for me in words I can't hear or understand. Thank You for listening to others' prayers for me and leading me forward in Your ways. Amen.

EVENING DEVOTION

We know about it now because of the coming of Jesus Christ, the One Who saves. He put a stop to the power of death and brought life that never dies which is seen through the Good News.
2 TIMOTHY 1:10

Jesus' death on the cross and His resurrection did away with death completely. For those who believe in Jesus, death can't touch them. When they die, they just shed their bodies here on earth and step through the doorway into everlasting life. When you die, you can be sure that Jesus will walk through that doorway with you, just as He has walked with you every day of your life.

BEYOND WHAT WE DESERVE
(Jeremiah 50:4–5)

MORNING PRAYER

Dear Jesus, be my guide. Take me through every twist and turn in the road ahead. Don't allow me to stray, to go off on my own way and leave You behind. I never want to leave or forget You. Forgive me for the times I have. Wash that sin away and make me new again so I can start fresh. Thank You, Jesus, for all You do for me. I love You. Amen.

EVENING DEVOTION

*If we have no faith, He will still be faithful
for He cannot go against what He is.*
2 TIMOTHY 2:13

We don't deserve what God gives us. Too often we are unfaithful and stumble through life. But thanks to Jesus, our lack of faith and our tendency to disobey God don't change the way He thinks about us. Jesus took away our sin, and because of this, God is good to us beyond anything we deserve. Even when we sin and are unfaithful to God, He remains faithful to us.

JEREMIAH 50:17–51:14
2 TIMOTHY 3
PROVERBS 14:28–35

REST IN HIM
(Proverbs 14:29)

MORNING PRAYER

Lord, I often need Proverbs 14:29. People upset me, and I'm ready to lose my temper. Please help me to be as slow to get angry as You are. Instead of letting anger well up inside me, I want to be understanding, patient, and caring. Those I'm upset with probably aren't having a good day either. Keep me from doing or saying something I'll end up being sorry for. Amen.

EVENING DEVOTION

The One Who saves and makes them free is strong.
The Lord of All is His name. He will work hard for
their cause, so that He may give rest to the land. But
He will not give rest to the people of Babylon.
JEREMIAH 50:34

There's no weakness that God can't strengthen. There's no fear He can't banish. There's no hurt He can't heal. There's no distress He can't relieve. There's no darkness He can't turn into light. There's no sorrow He can't turn into joyful dancing. This is your God. He loves you. Rest in Him.

STAND BY ME
(Proverbs 15:1–7)

MORNING PRAYER

God, there is such power in words. Forgive me when I abuse that power. When my words stir up anger, forgive me. Give me a gentle spirit to respond graciously when others speak in anger. Help me to speak with wisdom instead of foolishness. Let my words comfort others and build them up. And when I've said enough, remind me to be silent. Amen.

EVENING DEVOTION

But the Lord was with me. He gave me power to preach the Good News so all the people who do not know God might hear. I was taken from the mouth of the lion.

2 TIMOTHY 4:17

Jesus stands by us even though no one stood by Him in His hour of need. The way He felt forgotten and alone on the cross is something we could never imagine. We will never be turned away because Jesus was turned away that day on the cross. We will never be alone because He was. We will never suffer the punishment we deserve because He did. You can be sure Jesus will always stand by you—not because of anything you do, but because He loves you.

DAY 308

JEREMIAH 52–LAMENTATIONS 1
TITUS 1:1–9
PROVERBS 15:10–17

NOT EVEN A DROP
(Proverbs 15:16–17)

MORNING PRAYER

Lord, when I feel like putting up a fight, make me slow to anger. Help me choose what is better. Keep me calm when I feel irritated, and when trouble stirs, keep me from letting it grow. Fill me with Your Holy Spirit, and teach me how to choose the best way to ease whatever conflict comes my way. Amen.

EVENING DEVOTION

This truth also gives hope of life that lasts forever. God promised this before the world began. He cannot lie.
TITUS 1:2

God cannot lie. This means the promises He speaks in the Bible are always true and trustworthy. He has promised eternal life in heaven to His children. As a son of God, you have a true and sure hope of living forever with Him in heaven one day. Your life here on earth is like a drop of water in the ocean when compared to the perfectly joyful and blessed life that's waiting for you in heaven.

LIGHT YOUR WAY
(Titus 2:1–7)

MORNING PRAYER

Dear God, I thank You for the older men in my life who teach me. Not just teachers at school, but especially older men like a father, an uncle, or a grandfather. Thanks too for those at church who guide me. Remind me to be open to their teaching, to listen to their words, and to see them as role models for living a godly life. Bless them today, Lord. Amen.

EVENING DEVOTION

It is because of the Lord's loving-kindness that we are not destroyed for His loving-pity never ends. It is new every morning. He is so very faithful. "The Lord is my share," says my soul, "so I have hope in Him."
LAMENTATIONS 3:22–24

This passage in Lamentations 3 was written by someone who was suffering. That makes the words even more powerful. The author held on to faith even in his darkness, when his only hope was in God's faithfulness. No matter how dark your days are, you can be sure that God's light will find its way in and shine brightly on you. Don't ever forget how very much He loves you.

LAMENTATIONS 3:39–5:22
TITUS 3
PROVERBS 15:27–33

BEFORE YOU SPEAK
(Lamentations 3:55–58)

MORNING PRAYER

Lord God, sometimes I get so tired of negative stuff in my life that I find it hard to pray. Sometimes the only prayer I can offer is "Help!" and that's enough. You hear me. You run to me, comfort me, and take away my fear. You take that tiny prayer and turn it into a blessing. You always help me. Lord, I thank You and I praise You! Amen.

EVENING DEVOTION

The mind of the one who is right with God thinks about how to answer, but the mouth of the sinful pours out sinful things.
PROVERBS 15:28

"Think before you speak" may seem like a tired phrase, but still, it's a valuable one. A person who is right with God thinks about his answer before he replies. A person who doesn't know God says worthless things with no thought or care. Whose speech do your words resemble more—the one who is right with God or the one who doesn't know Him?

ULTIMATE GUIDE
(Philemon 14–17)

MORNING PRAYER

Lord, it must have been hard for Onesimus to return to Philemon, uncertain of how he would be received. It must be similar today for Christians who have lost their way. When they come back to You, are they worried other Christians might not accept them? And what about friends who have wronged me and are sorry? Teach me not to judge. Remind me to be kind to those who are sorry and want another chance. Amen.

EVENING DEVOTION

*The mind of a man plans his way, but
the Lord shows him what to do.*
PROVERBS 16:9

No matter what plans you make for how your life should go, God is the one who ultimately guides your steps. The story of Onesimus in the book of Philemon is just one example. Onesimus left Philemon as a runaway slave, but Paul suggested that he return to Philemon as a fellow brother in Christ. It's doubtful Onesimus had planned this for his life when he ran away. But the story God created for him was more glorious than anything he could have imagined.

TRULY FREE

(Proverbs 16:20)

MORNING PRAYER

Dear God, the better I understand the Bible, the more successful I can be. The more I study it, the more I learn about living. When I read Your Word, I don't have to worry about the future. You've already planned it for me. Your Word helps me make wise choices. As I go about my day today, remind me of the Bible verses I've memorized. Lead me to act in ways that please You. Amen.

EVENING DEVOTION

God was so good to make a way for us to be saved from the punishment of sin. . . . The Lord was the first to tell us of this. Then those who heard Him told it later. God proved what they said was true by showing us special things to see and by doing powerful works. He gave the gifts of the Holy Spirit as He wanted to.

HEBREWS 2:3–4

Proof of God is everywhere! We can't miss Him working in the lives of people. We see God turn those who hate Him into Christians who love Him. We see Him as the Creator of everything on earth and in the universe. And we can't forget God's power. People who don't know Him don't have the promise of eternal life. But those who accept Him are freed from their sin and promised life with Him forever in heaven. Spread this news to everyone you know.

MORE GLORIOUS
(Proverbs 16:31)

MORNING PRAYER

Heavenly Father, Proverbs 16:31 says white hair is like a crown of honor—a crown of years of wisdom. It's true, God, that wisdom comes with age. I've seen it in my family and friends. Older people have lived a long time, and they have years of wisdom. Older people give the best advice. Thank You, God, for the seniors in my life. Amen.

EVENING DEVOTION

It is true that we share the same Father with Jesus. And it is true that we share the same kind of flesh and blood because Jesus became a man like us. He died as we must die. Through His death He destroyed the power of the devil who has the power of death. Jesus did this to make us free from the fear of death. We no longer need to be chained to this fear.
HEBREWS 2:14–15

Maybe someone you loved has died. Maybe that made you afraid of dying. Put those thoughts away and live life joyfully without worry. Jesus has all your days planned, and someday when it's your time to go to heaven, He will gently lead you into a more glorious life. But today you are alive on this earth. Thank God for today. Enjoy it. Celebrate!

SPEAK UP
(Hebrews 3:13)

MORNING PRAYER

Dear God, when I see someone struggling with sin, show me how to offer encouragement and support. Teach me how to pray for that person. Help me to overcome my own struggles so I might be a better example. Fill my mind and heart with Your Word and Your Spirit. Don't allow my heart to be hardened by sin. Instead, fill it with so much of You that sin has no place to go. Amen.

EVENING DEVOTION

*He who laughs at the poor brings shame to his Maker.
He who is glad at trouble will be punished.*
PROVERBS 17:5

Throughout the Bible, we see God defending and loving the poor and needy. He's all about justice, and He pays special attention to those who are treated unfairly. Those who mistreat the poor and needy are really just mocking God, which is a very bad idea. Those who speak up for and defend the mistreated become more like God. They reflect His Spirit of fairness and love.

FAR FROM PERFECT
(Proverbs 17:9)

MORNING PRAYER

Father God, You always speak truth and love. You don't whisper bad things about me in the ears of others. I want to be more like You. Forgive me for when I've said unkind things about others or passed along gossip. I'm ashamed of that stuff. Remind me of how I've felt when people have said unkind things about me. Lead me to speak words to build others up, not tear them down. Amen.

EVENING DEVOTION

*Let us go with complete trust to the throne of God.
We will receive His loving-kindness and have His
loving-favor to help us whenever we need it.*
HEBREWS 4:16

How would you feel walking up to God as He sits on His throne? You are far from perfect. Would that make you afraid? God is forgiving and kind. Anything you've done to displease Him has already been forgiven through Jesus. God wants you to come to Him. Run to Him as a son would run to his dad. Come to God without fear every day. Tell Him your wants, needs, and troubles. Your loving Father is waiting for you, happy to hear your voice.

EZEKIEL 13–14
HEBREWS 5:11–6:20
PROVERBS 17:13–22

ANCHORED
(Hebrews 6:18–19)

MORNING PRAYER

Mighty God, Your promises in the Bible anchor me; they give me hope and strengthen my faith. You never change Your mind. Sometimes we have to wait patiently for Your promises to be fulfilled, but in Your own time, You always do exactly what You say. Your way is always the best way, right and true. Your promises last forever, even beyond life here on earth. Amen.

EVENING DEVOTION

This hope is a safe anchor for our souls. It will never move. This hope goes into the Holiest Place of All behind the curtain of heaven.
HEBREWS 6:19

A ship's anchor keeps the ship from breaking free. Our hope in God, our trust in His faithfulness, is like an anchor that keeps us close to Him. It gives us comfort in hard times because we know that God holds us steady and keeps us safe. Jesus' death on the cross anchored us to God forever. No matter how big the waves in our lives or how strong the winds, our hope in God brings us peace.

CONNECTED

(Hebrews 7:25-27)

MORNING PRAYER

Lord, I thank You for the word *Savior*. It connects me with You forever. You, Jesus—sinless and perfect in every way—took away all my sins by trading Your life for mine. That is so huge! You gave the world the enormous gift of Your sacrifice and saved us from the punishment for our sins. Thank You, Jesus! Thank You for the gift of eternal life in heaven. Amen.

EVENING DEVOTION

But Jesus lives forever. He is the Religious Leader forever. It will never change. And so Jesus is able, now and forever, to save from the punishment of sin all who come to God through Him because He lives forever to pray for them.
HEBREWS 7:24–25

Hebrews 7:25 says that Jesus prays for you. Think about that. Jesus, the Son of God, prays for you! Just as you pray for your family, friends, and others you care about, Jesus lifts you up in prayer, talking about you with His Father. You couldn't ask for a better prayer partner. Jesus knows you perfectly. He is firmly connected to you, understanding your every want and need. Just as He prayed for others when He lived here on earth, Jesus prays for you today.

GOD'S FAMILY
(Ezekiel 17:22–23)

MORNING PRAYER

Dear Father, the Bible says You took a young branch from a cedar tree and planted it. It grew into a powerful strong tree, providing food and shelter for birds. I think I'm like that new tree. You've planted me here with the purpose of growing up to be a strong Christian man who will serve You by helping others. God, feed me with Your Word. Help me to grow strong in my faith. Amen.

EVENING DEVOTION

"Now this was the sin of your sister Sodom: She and her daughters had pride, much food, and too much rest, but she did not help those who were poor and in need. They were proud and did hated sins in front of Me. So I took them away when I saw it."

EZEKIEL 16:49–50

In the Bible, Sodom was a sinful city. God accused the people there of having too much pride. They partied and were lazy. They didn't notice or care about those in their city who were in need. God did away with Sodom because of its sins. We are still sinful people, maybe not too different from those in Sodom. But thanks to Jesus, God will never get rid of us. Instead, if we have accepted Jesus as our Savior, God loves us and welcomes us into His family, making us pure and free of sin.

FAIR
(Ezekiel 18:5–9)

MORNING PRAYER

Dear God, I want to do what is right and good. That means taking responsibility and not selfishly wanting too much of anything. It means making good, clean choices. You want me to treat others well and to work at nurturing my relationships. I try, but I mess up a lot. Forgive me. When I don't know what to do, remind me to stop, think, and choose what is pleasing to You. Amen.

EVENING DEVOTION

*"Yet you say, 'The Lord is not doing what is right.'
Listen, O people of Israel! Is My way not right?
Is it not your ways that are not right?"*
EZEKIEL 18:25

Maybe you've thought that God isn't fair. Most of us have. But do we have a right to say that God's ways aren't fair? To begin with, we can't come close to understanding the plans He has for us. We've given God nothing compared to all the blessings He gives us. How many times have we put our wants ahead of His or followed our own ways instead of those He has set before us? Maybe *we're* the ones who are unfair.

DAY 320

EZEKIEL 20
HEBREWS 10:1–25
PROVERBS 18:18–24

PAID FOR
(Proverbs 18:24)

MORNING PRAYER

Heavenly Father, I want to thank You this morning for my friends. I don't know what I'd do without them. We have fun together, but we support each other too. Friends understand in ways others can't. You are my best friend, God—my friend above all other friends. Thank You for Your friendship. Thank You for the amazing friends You've brought into my life. Amen.

EVENING DEVOTION

But Christ gave Himself once for sins and that is good forever. After that He sat down at the right side of God.
HEBREWS 10:12

Jesus sat down at the right hand of God. His work was completed. It was finished. Jesus' sacrifice, giving His life for ours, was so powerful that it put an end to the need for any further sacrifices. His work on earth is finished, which means that your sins are already paid for. There is nothing you have done or ever will do that will take away His promise of forgiveness and eternal life.

HOLDING ON
(Hebrews 10:36)

MORNING PRAYER

Heavenly Father, patience isn't easy. I'm too often guilty of giving up. I guess I want what I want, and I want it now. Forgive me. Instead of giving up, I should just calm down and ask what You want me to do. You promise to guide me. So set me on the right path, God. Lead me to do Your work, and I will trust You with the outcome. Amen.

EVENING DEVOTION

*The very worst thing that can happen to a man
is to fall into the hands of the living God!*
HEBREWS 10:31

God is love. But thinking of Him only as a loving God is to limit your knowledge of Him and His power. God is the almighty ruler of the universe. Because of His greatness, He is worthy of respect and even fear. With a single word, God is able to destroy; just as quickly, with a single word, He is able to build. Don't lose sight of your respect for Him and the power He has over the world.

DAY 322

EZEKIEL 23
HEBREWS 11:1-31
PROVERBS 19:9-14

PROOF
(Hebrews 11:1)

MORNING PRAYER

Heavenly Father, although I can't see You, I know You exist. Thank You for the gift of faith. I pray for those who don't know You. Because they can't see You, they don't understand that You are capable of living inside their hearts and giving them a good life, not only here on earth but also forever in heaven. My prayer this morning is that You will lead them to Jesus. Amen.

EVENING DEVOTION

People who say these things show they are looking for a country of their own. . . . But they wanted a better country. And so God is not ashamed to be called their God. He has made a city for them.
HEBREWS 11:14, 16

Do your friends see your relationship with Jesus? Is He recognizable in your actions and words? Right now, you have a temporary home here on earth, in your country. But you are headed to a permanent home in heaven. Would you like your friends to be there with you? Then show them Jesus. Teach them that although He can't be seen with human eyes, He exists. Not only in heaven but on earth—today.

HOME IN HEAVEN
(Proverbs 19:21)

MORNING PRAYER

Dear God, I start each day with a plan. I always have at least an idea of what I'm going to do. But sometimes You step in and change everything. A phone call, a teacher's assignment, a friend getting sick—just one little change in plans affects my whole day. My plans might change, God, but Your plan is solid. So I give this day to You with only two words: lead me. Amen.

EVENING DEVOTION

They were too good for this world.
HEBREWS 11:38

Hebrews 11:38 ends with a small and important sentence: "They were too good for this world." Take time to read the whole chapter. Paul lists some of the people in the Bible whose faith was strong, people like Noah, Moses, Abraham, and Sarah. He writes about the troubles they had. These people didn't deserve their trouble, but God brought them through it. They knew that no matter what they suffered on earth, God had something amazing planned for their future: a home with Him forever in heaven.

EZEKIEL 27–28
HEBREWS 12:1–13
PROVERBS 19:22–29

CORRECTED

(Hebrews 12:1–2)

MORNING PRAYER

Jesus, You are like a coach preparing me for a race. With each step I take, You build my faith. You set up a goal for me. You stand at the finish line waiting for me, and I take off running. I want to overcome any obstacle that gets in the way of my reaching the finish line and coming home to You. Teach me, Lord. Coach me to run the best race. Amen.

EVENING DEVOTION

If you are not punished as all sons are, it means that you are not a true son of God. You are not a part of His family and He is not your Father.

HEBREWS 12:8

Maybe you think it would be great if your parents never corrected you. But then you would grow up without knowing right from wrong. God is like a good parent. Sometimes He corrects us to get us back on the right path. As He corrects us, God makes us more like Himself. Remember that He teaches and corrects you because You are one of His children. When you sense God telling you no, listen. Your perfect heavenly Father only wants what's best for you.

BUILD UP OTHERS
(Hebrews 12:14–15)

MORNING PRAYER

Dear Lord, sometimes I complain. I can have a bad attitude too—one that doesn't set a good example for others. I want to do better; I *know* I can do better. I want my attitude and my words to build people up. I want younger kids to look up to me as a good example of how a Christian should talk and act. Will You help me, please? Amen.

EVENING DEVOTION

Many men tell about their own loving-kindness and good ways but who can find a faithful man?
PROVERBS 20:6

Be careful not to become the kind of man who brags about being good. In that sort of person, goodness is often hard to find. Be someone who doesn't speak much of yourself. Instead, let your actions and character prove your faith in Jesus. Work hard at building people up. When someone praises you for your goodness, give the credit to God.

THE JOY HE OFFERS
(Hebrews 13)

MORNING PRAYER

Lord God, I praise You because nothing happens to me without Your permission. Everything I experience works together for my good and Your glory. Even on days when I feel out of sorts, I know You are with me, wanting what is best for me and working out the perfect plan You have for me. I praise You, God, not just today but every day, because You are so good. In You I find joy. Amen.

EVENING DEVOTION

It was the same with Jesus. He suffered and died outside the city so His blood would make the people clean from sin. So let us go to Him outside the city to share His shame.
HEBREWS 13:12–13

Have you ever felt like you didn't fit in? We've all found ourselves in uncomfortable situations, knowing we don't quite belong in the place where we find ourselves. Maybe someone has made you feel unwelcome because you are a Christian. Jesus' disciples felt that way. Jesus Himself was turned away by those who didn't believe He was the Son of God. If ever you feel unwelcome, remember that Jesus will always welcome you. Find joy in that truth. Jesus loves you. He will never turn you away.

THE NEEDY
(Ezekiel 33:30)

MORNING PRAYER

God, Ezekiel must have felt encouraged when people were eager to hear him speak about You. I hope when I talk with my friends about You, they will be just as ready to listen. Give me the right words to say. And if they won't accept my words or end up making fun of me, don't allow me to become discouraged. Draw me near to You and give me the courage to keep trying. God, they need You. Amen.

EVENING DEVOTION

Religion that is pure and good before God the Father is to help children who have no parents and to care for women whose husbands have died who have troubles. Pure religion is also to keep yourself clean from the sinful things of the world.
JAMES 1:27

How would you define "pure religion"—in other words, perfect devotion to God? James says pure religion is helping others and keeping yourself away from sin. That probably isn't the answer you came up with, but that is what God calls us to do. If you aren't helping others and doing your best to live in ways pleasing to God, is your heart where it should be? Think about whether you need to make some changes to more closely fit James' definition of pure religion.

EZEKIEL 34:11–36:15
JAMES 2
PROVERBS 21:1–8

IMITATE CHRIST
(James 2)

MORNING PRAYER

Heavenly Father, how I act should match what I say, and my words and my actions should please You. When I make an unkind comment, help me to be both humble and brave, and ask for forgiveness. When I act poorly, other people will not see God's love in my life. So please help me to speak and act more like Jesus. Guide me to speak with kindness and truth and to make good on my promises. Amen.

EVENING DEVOTION

A faith that does not do things is a dead faith.
JAMES 2:17

Jesus is always working for our good. As you try to be more like Him, be sure you put your faith in Him to work for others. Doing good works is one of the most obvious ways you can imitate Jesus. Think about the ways He helped the poor, those who needed strength and comfort and especially those who needed to know God. What can you do today to act more like Jesus? How can you put your faith to work by helping others?

THE LORD AT WORK
(Ezekiel 37:19–28)

MORNING PRAYER

Lord God, I don't like people to split apart because of their opinions. I wish we could all just get along. You have a way of bringing people together, so this morning, that is my prayer. Please, God, bring people together. Heal their differences. Help *Your* people especially to focus on You and love one another so we can make this world a much better place. Amen.

EVENING DEVOTION

"'I will put My Spirit within you, and you will come to life. I will place you in your own land. Then you will know that I, the Lord, have spoken and have done it,' says the Lord."
EZEKIEL 37:14

Ezekiel's book in the Bible might seem somewhat sad. But what stands out are the passages about God saving His people. Even when you feel sad, God's Spirit is alive and working within you. He doesn't leave His children alone in their sadness. When you feel down, God will lead you back to joy. Sometimes in those moments when you are sad or alone, you might feel nearer to God and sense Him at work in your heart.

WHAT YOU WANT
(James 4:1–3)

MORNING PRAYER

Dear God, forgive me for those times when I want what others have. You've blessed me with so much, and I'm truly grateful. Forgive me when I make my wants more important than what You desire for me. I know it's okay to ask for things in prayer, but when I ask, please lead me to ask according to Your will. Thank You, God. Amen.

EVENING DEVOTION

Or if you do ask, you do not receive because your reasons for asking are wrong. You want these things only to please yourselves.
JAMES 4:3

Sometimes we ask for something simply for our own selfish reasons without thinking about how it fits into God's plan or how it will affect others. We try to make God fit into our plans instead of us fitting into His. Would your prayers sound different if your greatest want was to be of use to God? Would your prayers sound different if your first thought was toward others rather than yourself?

DEEP ROOTS
(James 5:13–18)

MORNING PRAYER

Lord, when I join You for quiet time, I remember how important it is to pray. There is no situation where prayer isn't valuable. When I pray, I am more aware of the deep connection I have with You. I remember that You have power over everything. When I pray, I find healing, forgiveness, joy, and thankfulness for knowing You. I end this prayer with joyful praise. Amen.

EVENING DEVOTION

*You must be willing to wait also. Be strong in your
hearts because the Lord is coming again soon.*
JAMES 5:8

James says we are to make our hearts strong to get ready for Jesus coming back to earth. Just as a tree needs water and food from the earth to make its roots strong, your heart needs to become strong from reading God's Word. Your goal is a deeper, stronger relationship with Jesus. Talk with Him in your daily prayers. Make knowing Him better the most important thing in your life.

HEAVENLY REWARD

(Proverbs 22:6)

MORNING PRAYER

Heavenly Father, I want to thank You this morning for all the adults who have helped to raise me. I haven't always been grateful. Sometimes I've disagreed with them and even rebelled. I know they want the best for me, and that's a life with You in my heart. They led me to meet Jesus and to accept Him as my Savior. Bless my parents today and all the other helpers in my life. Amen.

EVENING DEVOTION

We will receive the great things that we have been promised. They are being kept safe in heaven for us. They are pure and will not pass away. They will never be lost. You are being kept by the power of God because you put your trust in Him and you will be saved from the punishment of sin at the end of the world.

1 PETER 1:4–5

Have you ever wondered what heaven is like? Peter says God has great things safely stored there for us just waiting for the day we arrive. We can't imagine what those things are, but we know they are perfect in every way. Until then, we wait and put all our faith and trust in God that at the end of our lives, He will give us everything He has promised.

HOLY
(1 Peter 2:1–3)

MORNING PRAYER

Dear Jesus, some days I'm not sure of who I am. My feelings are all over the place. I mess up a lot too. Sometimes sin isn't something I see clearly until I'm in the middle of it. When I read my Bible, open my eyes to a fuller understanding of sin. You are holy and good, and I know if I put my trust in You, You will help me. Amen.

EVENING DEVOTION

Be holy in every part of your life. Be like the Holy One Who chose you. The Holy Writings say, "You must be holy, for I am holy."
1 PETER 1:15–16

What does it mean to be holy? It means to work at becoming more like Jesus. Of course, He is the only one who is perfectly holy and free from sin. Your task is to spend each day learning more about Him and then putting what you've learned into action. Holiness is a lifelong process. God asks you to become as holy as you can be here on earth until that day when He makes you perfect in heaven.

EZEKIEL 45–46
1 PETER 2:4–17
PROVERBS 22:24–29

UPRIGHT
(1 Peter 2:12–15)

MORNING PRAYER

Lord, You remind me that I have to be super aware of how I act around those who don't know You. Sometimes those are the very people I want to avoid, the loud ones who cause fights, get into trouble, and use bad language. Yet these are the people You most want to reach. So, God, through my actions and words help me to be the best example to show them who You are. Amen.

EVENING DEVOTION

Show respect to all men. Love the Christians. Honor God with love and fear. Respect the head leader of the country.
1 PETER 2:17

First Peter 2:17 offers simple advice about how we should live. Peter says to be respectful. He adds that Christians should come together in love for each other and for God. We are also to honor God. That means loving God and recognizing the great power He has over the universe. Finally, we should show respect when dealing with those who have authority over us: parents, teachers, and all leaders. We should be good citizens—the best citizens we can be while still obeying God and His laws.

THE LORD IS THERE
(Proverbs 23:9)

MORNING PRAYER

Dear Jesus, when I try to tell some of my friends about You, they don't want to listen. Then I find myself getting upset and defensive. Maybe those who won't listen aren't ready to accept You yet. Will You please guide me to those who *are* ready? Teach me to speak about You at just the right times and with just the right words. Thank You, Lord. Amen.

EVENING DEVOTION

"It will be 9,000 long steps around the city. And the name of the city from that time on will be: 'The Lord is there.'"
EZEKIEL 48:35

"The Lord is there" is a strange name for a city, but it's a wonderful name, isn't it? The words "The Lord is there" would always remind its citizens that God is with them, living right there among them. God is always with you too. You could name your heart "The Lord is there" because He lives in your heart now and will continue to live there every day for the rest of your life.

ATTITUDE OF PRAISE
(Daniel 2:17–23)

MORNING PRAYER

Dear God, You are the answer to all my prayers, the *yes* to all my needs. Daniel said, "I give thanks and praise to You, O God of my fathers" (Daniel 2:23). I echo Daniel's praise. You give me wisdom and strength. You also give me the courage to speak about You and to stand up for what I know is right. I praise You, "O God of my fathers," and I thank You. Amen.

EVENING DEVOTION

Then the secret was made known to Daniel in a special dream during the night. He gave honor and thanks to the God of heaven.

DANIEL 2:19

When God answered Daniel's prayer, the first thing Daniel did was praise Him. How often do you remember to praise God after He has answered a prayer? Maybe you forget that God gets credit for the answer, not you. We should always remember to praise and thank God. All the time He is providing us with things we didn't even think to ask for. God deserves the credit. Every good thing in our lives is a gift from Him.

EVEN IF. . .
(Daniel 3:16–18)

MORNING PRAYER

Lord, I want faith like that of Shadrach, Meshach, and Abed-nego. Even when things got really bad, they didn't lose faith in You. They refused to give in to fear. They trusted You to get them through a very frightening situation—and You did bring them through it! This morning, I ask You to build up my faith. As I go about today, I will remember that You are the one who makes me strong. Amen.

EVENING DEVOTION

*He said, "Look! I see four men loose and walking about
in the fire without being hurt! And the fourth one
looks like a son of the gods (or the Son of God)!"*
DANIEL 3:25

The story of Shadrach, Meshach, and Abed-nego is an example of how Jesus is with us even in the worst circumstances. He never leaves us alone to fight against fear. We can't see Him with our eyes, but we can be certain He is standing next to us, helping us and giving us courage and strength. The next time you wonder how you'll make it through a difficult situation, remember Shadrach, Meshach, and Abed-nego. Jesus is with you, just as He was with them.

ALL YOU NEED
(2 Peter 1:3–8)

MORNING PRAYER

Heavenly Father, You have given me everything I need. Above all, You are helping me understand who You are and how You want me to live. You are adding to my character, building me up in goodness, knowledge, self-control, patience, and love. Each day as I practice these things, I become more like You. Thank You, Lord, for meeting all my needs and forming me into the person You want me to be. Amen.

EVENING DEVOTION

"But at the end of that time I, Nebuchadnezzar, looked up toward heaven and my understanding returned to me. And I gave thanks to the Most High and praised and honored Him Who lives forever. For His nation lasts forever, and His rule is for all people for all time."

DANIEL 4:34

As prisoners in Babylon, God's people likely felt that God had left them or that they had somehow messed up His plan. They couldn't have known that God would use their situation to bring an evil king into a relationship with Him. We can't know what God plans to do through the trouble He allows in our lives. But we should always trust in His power and believe He has a better plan than ours.

TEST THE TEACHING
(Proverbs 24:1–18)

MORNING PRAYER

God, I wish I had Your eyes. So often I don't see the needs of others. I don't always see sadness, worry, or a lack of confidence. I often just see the good stuff. Worse, I even want what others have or feel glad when someone I dislike fails. Forgive me, God! Open my eyes to others' needs. Help me to focus on helping them and on living a life that pleases You. Amen.

EVENING DEVOTION

Such people are like wells without water. They are like clouds before a storm. The darkest place below has been kept for them.
2 PETER 2:17

Be careful of false teaching—twisting God's words to make them mean something they don't. False teaching always leads you down the wrong path. Test what others say about God or certain issues to be sure it lines up with what's in the Bible. If it doesn't, reject it. If you aren't sure, then ask God to help You understand. He hates false teaching, and He wants you to live by the true Word of God. Read your Bible every day, study it, and learn.

DANIEL 6:1–7:14
2 PETER 3
PROVERBS 24:19–27

PRICE OF PRAYER
(Daniel 6:1–13)

MORNING PRAYER

Dear God, in some parts of the world, praying to You in public isn't allowed. People have to worship You in secret. I can't imagine, God, being punished for praying and believing in You. This morning, I pray for all those who can't gather to worship and praise You. I ask that You protect them and keep them from being punished for their faith. Amen.

EVENING DEVOTION

Then these men said, "We will not find anything to say against Daniel unless it has to do with the Law of his God."
DANIEL 6:5

The only way Daniel's enemies could trap him was to accuse him of praying when the king had made a rule against it. Daniel's only "crime" was prayer! His enemies couldn't find anything else to accuse him of. Daniel lived a godly life, and his faith in God couldn't be bent. He obeyed all the rules the king set, except one—Daniel wouldn't bow to any other god. He wouldn't stop praying and worshiping the one true God. If you were in Daniel's situation, would you have done the same?

RULE OF LOVE
(1 John 1:7–2:17)

MORNING PRAYER

Dear God, stop me when worldly things take Your place in my heart. I want to love people, not things. I want to love them as You do, giving of myself, placing their needs ahead of my own. And I want my love to be like a shining light that leads them to You. Show me how to do that. Teach me to love others with Your kind of love. Amen.

EVENING DEVOTION

If we say that we have no sin, we lie to ourselves and the truth is not in us. If we tell Him our sins, He is faithful and we can depend on Him to forgive us of our sins. He will make our lives clean from all sin.
1 JOHN 1:8–9

There is no reason not to tell your sins to God. If you don't tell Him your sins, you're basically pretending they don't exist. Denying your sin leaves a nagging feeling in your heart that something's not right. Remember, God has already forgiven you. Even so, it's important to come to Him in truth and admit that you messed up. And you should never worry or be afraid to tell Him. He loves you.

DANIEL 9–10
1 JOHN 2:18–29
PROVERBS 25:1–12

JUSTICE
(Proverbs 25:2)

MORNING PRAYER

Dear Lord, *justice* is a word we hear a lot. It means fair treatment. Sometimes we're too quick to judge one another. Your judgments are always based on truth. I pray, this morning, that everyone who wants to judge will be more like You. You are the final judge of everyone and everything. The more we learn about You, the fairer we will be with others. Amen.

EVENING DEVOTION

*"So the Lord brought trouble upon us. For the
Lord our God is right and good in all He does,
but we have not obeyed His voice."*
DANIEL 9:14

God is perfect. There's no place in His kingdom for sin. That's why we need to be rid of sin before we enter heaven. God is the King of justice. He knew we weren't capable of living life without sin, so instead of punishing us for our sins, He sent His Son, Jesus, to take the punishment we deserved. We should be so grateful to God for His mercy. We are forgiven the minute we accept Jesus as our Savior, and that forgiveness lasts forever.

FOREVER BELONGING

(1 John 3:1–3)

MORNING PRAYER

Dear God, thank you for calling me Your child. Living as a Christian is helping me to grow into a faithful and selfless man. Each day I change a little to become more like Jesus. Someday, I will meet You face-to-face. In the meantime, I am strengthened by Your love and forgiveness. I put my trust in You and I will follow Your Son, Jesus. Amen.

EVENING DEVOTION

See what great love the Father has for us that He would call us His children. And that is what we are. For this reason the people of the world do not know who we are because they did not know Him.

1 JOHN 3:1

You can almost sense the amazement in John's words at the idea of being called a child of God. We should all be amazed that the Creator of the universe would gift us with the honor and privilege of being one of His children. He sent Jesus, who released us from our sins and promised us eternal life in heaven. But God didn't stop there. He adopted us. We are His forever. His love is so great that it's impossible to understand.

DAY 344

HOSEA 1–3
1 JOHN 3:13–4:16
PROVERBS 25:18–28

RUN TO HIM
(Hosea 2:20–3:5)

MORNING PRAYER

Jesus, You call me and I run to You. Each morning You give me hope. On bad days, I know You will comfort me. It's like you're putting your arm around my shoulder and saying, "I'm always with you, son." I want Your loving-kindness and care. The more I read my Bible and learn about You, the more I understand Your love. Today, Jesus, I will tell others about You. I want them to know You too. Amen.

EVENING DEVOTION

"I will promise to make you Mine forever. Yes, I will take you as My bride in what is right and good and fair, and in loving-kindness and in loving-pity. I will keep My promise and make you Mine. Then you will know the Lord."
HOSEA 2:19–20

Maybe one day you will fall in love and become a husband. What would you expect from your wife? That she would be faithful to you, right? Faithfulness is key to a good marriage. Hosea 2:19 says God is like a good husband. He promises His love to you forever. He makes you His own. Even if you left Him a hundred times, He would lovingly take you back. God loves you even when it seems you don't deserve His love. Run to Him. He's waiting.

OVERCOMING
(Hosea 6)

MORNING PRAYER

Heavenly Father, every morning I come in prayer, wanting to know more of You. As I learn, I grow stronger in my faith. I hope I'll never get tired of learning from You. Teach me today. Show me all the little things I've missed. I will find You everywhere, if only I look for You. Help me to overcome whatever gets in my way. I'm ready, Lord. Let's go. Amen.

EVENING DEVOTION

*Every child of God has power over the sins of the world.
The way we have power over the sins of the world is
by our faith. Who could have power over the world
except by believing that Jesus is the Son of God?*
1 JOHN 5:4–5

Because of our faith in Jesus, we have overcome the world. This means that nothing on earth can touch us. No problem is so tough that it could come close to pulling us away from Jesus or darkening the light of His presence in our hearts. Jesus overcame every kind of evil. Since He lives in us, we have become overcomers as well.

NOT TAKEN LIGHTLY

(Hosea 10:11–12)

MORNING PRAYER

Heavenly Father, keep my thoughts set on You. Put me to work. I want to work by Your side, doing whatever job You have for me today. I'm not sure what it will be, but I trust You to bring me to it. With Your Spirit moving through me, I will do my best, and I will do it with goodness, kindness, and love in my heart. And whatever I accomplish, the credit goes to You. Amen.

EVENING DEVOTION

*Like a crazy man who throws pieces of burning wood
and arrows of death, so is the man who fools his
neighbor with a lie, and says, "I was only joking."*
PROVERBS 26:18–19

When you read the book of Proverbs, do you see that not much has changed about our behavior since long ago when the Bible was written? Do you see yourself in any of its sayings? Solomon warned against people who are rude and hurtful to someone and then cover themselves by saying, "I was only joking." Maybe you know someone like that. Bad behavior is never a joke.

WHAT IS GOOD
(3 John)

MORNING PRAYER

Father God, John's prayer for Gaius sounds like my short prayers when I think about my friends. I pray that they are doing well and feeling well. Sometimes I wonder if my short prayers about little things are okay with You. After reading John's prayer, I'm sure my prayers are fine. I also pray that my friends will know You. I want them to have everything good, and that begins with You. Amen.

EVENING DEVOTION

Dear friend, do not follow what is sinful, but follow what is good. The person who does what is good belongs to God. The person who does what is sinful has not seen God.

3 JOHN 11

When you do good, you are like God, because God is good, and He only does what is good for His people. Surround yourself with people who are already doing good and working hard for God's kingdom. Imitate these people. By imitating others who are already living in a way that honors God, you are really imitating Christ. The more Christlike you become, the more aware you are of evil and the more wholeheartedly you will want to do good.

DAY 348

JOEL 1:1–2:17
JUDE
PROVERBS 27:10–17

FREE FROM ALL SIN
(Joel 1:14)

MORNING PRAYER

Mighty God, I'm grateful for the Bible and its history. Its stories tell Your story and guide us in how we should live. I pray that everyone all over the world will read the Bible and know You. Send them Your Holy Spirit. Bring back those who have run away from You. I want everyone to know that thanks to Jesus they can be forgiven of their sins and live in heaven forever. Amen.

EVENING DEVOTION

There is One Who can keep you from falling and can bring you before Himself free from all sin. He can give you great joy as you stand before Him in His shining-greatness. He is the only God. He is the One Who saves from the punishment of sin through Jesus Christ our Lord.
JUDE 24–25

God is able to keep you from "falling"—from slipping into a life of sin. When you meet Him in heaven someday, thanks to Jesus you will stand before God free from all sin. And you will stand before Him with joy. You can be sure about that. Jesus says it's so. Accepting Him as your Savior means that even when you mess up, God will forgive you. Not just once or twice, but forever.

FIRST LOVE
(Revelation 2:1–4)

MORNING PRAYER

Dear God, forgive me for not always being aware of Your presence. When I first met You, I felt Your incredible love. Now, God, You've become like an old friend. I love You, but sometimes I don't feel as excited about loving You as I once did. I'm sorry. Please fill my heart to overflowing with a love for You that's always brand new. Amen.

EVENING DEVOTION

The Lord God says, "I am the First and the Last, the beginning and the end of all things. I am the All-powerful One Who was and Who is and Who is to come."
REVELATION 1:8

God is the First and the Last, the beginning and the ending of history. He has always existed. God has always been with you, and He will be your first and last love. He loved you even before you were born. He will love you still when you go to be with Him in heaven. Throughout your lifetime, you might fall in and out of love with people, but you will never have a day when God falls out of love with you.

AMOS 1:1–4:5
REVELATION 2:12–29
PROVERBS 28:1–8

FAITHFUL CHURCH

(Proverbs 28:1)

MORNING PRAYER

Lord God, bullies might seem tough, but to You they are made of straw. You give me power to stand up to those who don't like me. I'm not afraid of them, and I won't let them get to me. I'm Your child! I stand up strong, proud, and confident because of You. Today, God, I will be brave. No one can hurt me because I am Yours. Amen.

EVENING DEVOTION

"I know where you live. It is the place where Satan sits. I know that you are true to Me. You did not give up and turn away from your faith in Me, even when Antipas was killed. He was faithful in speaking for Me. He was killed in front of you where Satan is."

REVELATION 2:13

In today's passage, God's Spirit congratulated the church of Pergamum for holding on to their faith in Him even though sin was all around them. God's people—His church—remained faithful to Him when everyone else had rejected Him. The church stood up against evil. They proclaimed that God ruled the earth even in those places where Satan declared himself king.

LASTING WEALTH
(Amos 5:14–15)

MORNING PRAYER

Heavenly Father, the Bible shows me that people through-out history have had the same troubles. Things always came between You and them. I'm no different. I sometimes ignore You even though You are my friend—my best friend! Forgive me. Make me more like You. Give me a heart that hates evil and loves good. Let me put You front and center in my life so nothing will come between us. Amen.

EVENING DEVOTION

"You say that you are rich and that you need nothing, but you do not know that you are so troubled in mind and heart. You are poor and blind and without clothes."
REVELATION 3:17

What do you think it means to be rich? Sometimes wealth on earth makes us feel safe and secure. But the only true safety and security come from putting all our faith in God. He is our silver and gold—our everything! We are rich in His love and caring for us. He blesses us with things here on earth, but He has stored a treasure in heaven for us that is far beyond anything we can imagine.

AMOS 7–9
REVELATION 4:1–5:5
PROVERBS 28:17–24

INSPIRED TO PRAISE

(Amos 9:14–15)

MORNING PRAYER

God, You are so good to me. When I'm not successful, when I don't win, I know it's because You have something even better waiting for me. Maybe it's something I need to learn, or it might be an even more important task or event that I'll do well with. When I'm disappointed, I still praise You because I know You'll pick me up and start me on a new path to something good. Amen.

EVENING DEVOTION

*Each one of the four living beings had six wings.
They had eyes all over them, inside and out. Day
and night they never stop saying, "Holy, holy, holy
is the Lord God, the All-powerful One. He is the
One Who was and Who is and Who is to come."*

REVELATION 4:8

Imagine the "beings" in today's passage praising God, saying, "Holy, holy, holy is the Lord God, the All-powerful One. He is the One Who was and Who is and Who is to come." They never stop praising. Their heavenly job is to praise God. How often do you praise Him? You can't speak of His greatness all day long, but just by looking around at everything He has created and all the ways He has blessed you, you should have plenty of reasons to praise Him.

THE LION AND THE LAMB
(Obadiah)

MORNING PRAYER

God, I'm grateful to call You my Father. Keep me from repeating the same mistakes. When You rescue me from my problems, You teach me. You forgive me and give me a clean heart so I can have a fresh start. As I learn from You, I pass along to others what I learn. The more I talk about You, the more I want to learn about You. Thank You, Father, for Your never-ending love. Amen.

EVENING DEVOTION

I saw a Lamb standing in front of the twenty-four leaders. He was before the throne and in front of the four living beings. He looked as if He had been killed. He had seven horns and seven eyes. These are the seven Spirits of God. They have been sent out into all the world.

REVELATION 5:6

In his vision, John was told the Lion of Judah had authority to open the mysterious book. We think John will see this Lion, but what does he see instead? A dead lamb. A sad scene? Not when it's a symbol of Jesus. God (the Lion) loved us so much that He allowed His Son (the Lamb) to die in our place. The beauty is that Jesus came back to life. He lives today and one day we will live with Him in heaven.

MICAH 1:1–4:5
REVELATION 6:1–7:8
PROVERBS 29:1–8

NO PLACE FOR FEAR
(Revelation 7:4–8)

MORNING PRAYER

Dear God, when I read the book of Revelation, there's so much I don't understand. But maybe that's okay. You know all the answers to what will happen in the future. I only need to trust You. For now, I'm a member of Your tribe. I'm a son of God. Lead me into the future and place me exactly where You want me. My hope is to serve you for the rest of my life. Amen.

EVENING DEVOTION

*Every man will sit under his vine and under his
fig tree, with no one to make him afraid. For
the mouth of the Lord of All has spoken.*
MICAH 4:4

Micha 4:4 provides us with a powerful image of everyone sitting peacefully under a tree. The Lord has made them unafraid. Nothing can touch them. They're just sitting calmly, joyfully, in perfect peace. Everyone is afraid sometimes. But through our faith in God, we can find peace. No matter what scares us, God is bigger, and He has power over everything. Someday when we get to heaven, we'll have the perfectly unafraid kind of peace we see in this verse from the book of Micah.

HE'S DONE THE REST
(Micah 6:8)

MORNING PRAYER

Dear God, some mornings I ask, "God, what do You want me to do today?" I shouldn't ask. I already know the answer. You want me to make the right choices in the way I treat others. You want me to follow You as my role model. When I succeed at something, You want me to give the credit to You. If I do my best to please You, You will take care of the rest. Amen.

EVENING DEVOTION

What should I bring to the Lord when I bow down before the God on high? Should I come to Him with burnt gifts, with calves a year old? Will the Lord be pleased with thousands of rams, or with 10,000 rivers of oil? Should I give my first-born to pay for not obeying? Should I give the fruit of my body for the sin of my soul? O man, He has told you what is good. What does the Lord ask of you but to do what is fair and to love kindness, and to walk without pride with your God?
MICAH 6:6–8

In Bible times, people tried to pay for their sins. They made offerings to God and gave Him the best of their best. Think about this: God gave us the best of *His* best—His only Son, Jesus. In return, He asks nothing from us but to do what is right and good. We don't have to pay for our sins because Jesus already did. The next time you mess up, ask God to forgive You. That's all. Jesus will take care of the rest.

SAFE PLACE
(Nahum 1)

MORNING PRAYER

Almighty God, how great is Your goodness! I'm thankful for all the blessings You give me. I'm grateful too for the many times You've comforted me when I was sad. You take care of me, and I know You love me. You provide for all my needs and keep me safe. Nothing can hurt me as long as I hold tightly to You. I just wanted to say thank You this morning, God. Amen.

EVENING DEVOTION

Who can stand before His anger? Who can live through the burning of His anger? His anger is poured out like fire, and the rocks are broken up by Him. The Lord is good, a safe place in times of trouble. And He knows those who come to Him to be safe.

NAHUM 1:6–7

The book of Nahum starts out showing God's power against evil nations. It gives us a good picture of how fierce His power is. Any sort of evil had better not get in God's way because He will destroy it. But later in Nahum, we see a different side of God, how good and loving He is to His people. When trouble surrounds us, God is our safe place. He cares for those who trust in Him.

JOY IN JESUS
(Habakkuk 3:17–19)

MORNING PRAYER

Dear Jesus, my Savior, Your goodness, kindness, and love toward me don't change when my circumstances change. You never change. You keep on loving me just as I am, unconditionally. Whether things are going great or not so good, I praise You because of who You are. You are my strength. You make me strong. I trust You Jesus, and in You I find much joy. Amen.

EVENING DEVOTION

Even if the fig tree does not grow figs and there is no fruit on the vines, even if the olives do not grow and the fields give no food, even if there are no sheep within the fence and no cattle in the cattle-building, yet I will have joy in the Lord. I will be glad in the God Who saves me.
HABAKKUK 3:17–18

Habakkuk found his way through all kinds of trouble. Was this because he was especially powerful or well-off or had supportive friends? No. It was because whatever the circumstances, Habakkuk chose to rejoice in the Lord. God was more important to him than anything else. Good days. Bad days. It didn't matter. Habakkuk praised God just because of who God is. Habakkuk always found joy in his relationship with the Lord.

ZEPHANIAH
REVELATION 12
PROVERBS 30:1–6

WITH SINGING
(Zephaniah 3:17)

MORNING PRAYER

Lord God, do You really sing happy songs about me? That's what Zephaniah says. You have joy over me with loud singing! I wish I could hear that. Someday in heaven I will sing to You. Maybe we will even sing together. But until then, God, I am delighted that You care so much about me. I love You, heavenly Father. Amen.

EVENING DEVOTION

The Lord your God is with you, a Powerful One Who wins the battle. He will have much joy over you. With His love He will give you new life. He will have joy over you with loud singing.
ZEPHANIAH 3:17

The Lord rejoices over you with singing. Can you believe that? Can you imagine that the God who created the universe, holds it together, and listens to the prayers of billions of people rejoices over you? People might let you down and make you feel small and worthless, but when that happens, never forget that God continues to rejoice over you with joy and songs.

RELY ON HIM
(Haggai 2)

MORNING PRAYER

God, past and present are the same to You. You created time, and sometimes I forget that Your idea of time isn't the same as mine. Your promises don't change because of time. What the Bible says will happen in the future will happen—it's already done. Whatever I see around me, I know You have something even better waiting for me in heaven. Until then, I will live to please You and praise You. Amen.

EVENING DEVOTION

Two things I have asked of You. Do not keep me from having them before I die: Take lies and what is false far from me. Do not let me be poor or rich. Feed me with the food that I need.
PROVERBS 30:7–8

God is kind enough to give us just the right amount of earthly blessings—material things—so we will continue to rely on Him. Because He loves us, He always grants us contentment no matter what situation we find ourselves in. Our goal should be not so much to get ahead in life as to live life satisfied with whatever God gives us.

ZECHARIAH 1–4
REVELATION 14:14–16:3
PROVERBS 30:17–20

SMALL BEGINNINGS

(Revelation 15:2–4)

MORNING PRAYER

Dear God, Your kindness is beyond my understanding. Even when I can't see You at work, I know You are working out Your plan for me. You are always fair and right. You are the one and only God, and nothing on earth even comes close to who You are. Right now, all I see is the beginning of the wonderful things You have waiting for me. God, I praise You! Amen.

EVENING DEVOTION

"Who has hated the day of small things? Men will be glad when they see Zerubbabel building the walls of the Lord's house. These seven are the eyes of the Lord which travel over all the earth."

ZECHARIAH 4:10

Do not hate, or dislike, small things. Do you imagine what you want to do for God, and then when you think about it some more, you decide it seems too small or even worthless? God uses small things to make bigger things happen. Nothing you do for Him is ever too little. Think about something simple you can do for Him today, something like telling one friend about Jesus. Then each day, add to those small things you do. Watch them grow into something bigger.

GOD'S FINGERPRINTS

(Zechariah 8)

MORNING PRAYER

Dear God, I am one of Your people because You are my God. You are so good and faithful to me. I haven't done anything to deserve Your love and care for me. I know the only way to show my gratitude is to live in a way that pleases You and to serve You. How can I help others today, God? Work through me. Lead me in Your ways. Amen.

EVENING DEVOTION

There are four things that are small on the earth, but they are very wise: The ants are not a strong people, but they store up their food in the summer. The badgers are not a strong people, but they make their houses in the rocks. The locusts have no king, but they go as an army. You can take the lizard in your hands, but it is found in kings' houses.
PROVERBS 30:24–28

God's fingerprints are all over His creation. His character can be found in His creativity. Since He is the author of all living things, it makes sense that even the smallest of creatures—like ants, locusts, and lizards—can teach us about His wisdom. Take time to look around you. Learn from the powerful creation God has given you to enjoy.

STRONG CITY OF HOPE
(Zechariah 9:12)

MORNING PRAYER

Almighty God, I'm blessed to be a citizen living in Your "strong city of hope." It's that place in my heart where all Your promises are stored—the place where You live. Today's verse in Zechariah reminds me that some Christians might leave You, but even if they do, You are ready to welcome them back. You celebrate their return. I never want to leave You, God. I'm content with You right where I am. Amen.

EVENING DEVOTION

"These kings will fight and make war with the Lamb. But the Lamb will win the war because He is Lord of lords and King of kings. His people are the called and chosen and faithful ones."
REVELATION 17:14

Today's reading in Revelation says that evil will always be at war against Jesus. While that's true, there's good news: Jesus will always win over evil. Don't allow yourself to believe otherwise when evil seems to conquer good. God is always in control. Battles, small fights, will happen, but in the end, Jesus wins the war.

A VOICE
(Proverbs 31:4–9)

MORNING PRAYER

Dear Jesus, Proverbs 31:8 tells me to be the voice for those who can't speak and to speak up for the rights of those without help. When I see kids being picked on at school, help me to stand up for them. Give me courage to speak up in support of what is good and right. Give me the words, Lord. Help me to know when to speak and what to say. Amen.

EVENING DEVOTION

Open your mouth for those who cannot speak, and for the rights of those who are left without help. Open your mouth. Be right and fair in what you decide. Stand up for the rights of those who are suffering and in need.
PROVERBS 31:8–9

You are the voice for those who don't have one. Here on earth, you can be like the arms of Jesus reaching out to those who need help. You can speak up against injustice. You can judge everyone fairly without regard to social status, wealth, age, race, or gender. That's what our heavenly Father does. You can stand up for the poor and needy so they don't get left behind. Don't be afraid to speak up for what's right. God is on your side.

HEAVEN'S ARMIES
(Malachi 2:16)

MORNING PRAYER

Dear God, in Malachi 2:16 You say, "I hate divorce." I hate it too. I wish everyone's mom and dad would stay together. But that doesn't always happen. You are the God who forgives and allows second chances. I pray this morning for everyone affected by divorce. Heal broken hearts, Lord, and help people, divorced and otherwise, to love each other and get along. Amen.

EVENING DEVOTION

The coat He wears has been put in blood. His name is The Word of God. The armies in heaven were dressed in clean, white, fine linen. They were following Him on white horses.
REVELATION 19:13–14

Today's reading from Revelation shows the image of Jesus riding on a horse, ready to do battle against evil. His blood-stained robe reminds us of His death on the cross. Following Jesus is a heavenly army dressed in clean white linen and riding on white horses. The color white stands for purity. Christians on earth are like that army. They were made clean and pure when they accepted Jesus into their hearts. If you've accepted Christ as your Savior, you are a part of His army.

FOREVER
(Revelation 22)

MORNING PRAYER

Dear Jesus, You have always existed. You will be there at the end of my life and then forever with me in heaven. Someday You will return to earth and save it from all evil. But for now, You live in my heart. You will be with me through all eternity, Lord. I love You and praise You! Amen.

EVENING DEVOTION

I heard a loud voice coming from heaven. It said, "See! God's home is with men. He will live with them. They will be His people. God Himself will be with them. He will be their God. God will take away all their tears. There will be no more death or sorrow or crying or pain. All the old things have passed away."
REVELATION 21:3–4

Congratulations! You've reached the end of your 365-day Bible study. You've learned that God has existed forever. Someday this world will come to an end. When that happens, God will be there in total control. God will gather all His people together. There will be no more death. Everything will be made good, right, and perfect forever. Jesus says He's coming again, and we should look forward to His arrival. The Bible ends with this simple three-word prayer: "Come, Lord Jesus." Yes, Jesus is coming. You can be sure it's true!

SCRIPTURE INDEX

REVELATION

ANOTHER GREAT DEVOTIONAL FOR GUYS!

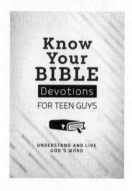

You want your life to matter, and *Know Your Bible Devotions for Teen Guys* encourages you to pursue greatness—by knowing and obeying God's Word. This entertaining and encouraging devotional addresses 101 topics vital to a life of Christian integrity, such as knowing God, following Jesus, prayer, encouragement, identity, purpose, and stewardship.

Paperback / ISBN 978-1-63609-630-8

Find This and More from Barbour
Publishing at Your Favorite Bookstore
or www.barbourbooks.com